ABOUT ISLAND PRESS

Island Press is the only nonprofit organization in the United States whose principal purpose is the publication of books on environmental issues and natural resource management. We provide solutions-oriented information to professionals, public officials, business and community leaders, and concerned citizens who are shaping responses to environmental problems.

In 2005, Island Press celebrates its twenty-first anniversary as the leading provider of timely and practical books that take a multidisciplinary approach to critical environmental concerns. Our growing list of titles reflects our commitment to bringing the best of an expanding body of literature to the environmental community throughout North America and the world.

Support for Island Press is provided by the Agua Fund, The Geraldine R. Dodge Foundation, Doris Duke Charitable Foundation, Ford Foundation, The George Gund Foundation, The William and Flora Hewlett Foundation, Kendeda Sustainability Fund of the Tides Foundation, The Henry Luce Foundation, The John D. and Catherine T. MacArthur Foundation, The Andrew W. Mellon Foundation, The Curtis and Edith Munson Foundation, The New-Land Foundation, The New York Community Trust, Oak Foundation, The Overbrook Foundation, The David and Lucile Packard Foundation, The Winslow Foundation, and other generous donors.

The opinions expressed in this book are those of the author(s) and do not necessarily reflect the views of these foundations.

THE
SUSTAINABLE
COMPANY

How to Create Lasting Value Through
Social and Environmental Performance

✦

CHRIS LASZLO

ISLANDPRESS

WASHINGTON — COVELO — LONDON

First Island Press cloth edition, September 2003
First Island Press paperback edition, July 2005

Published in cooperation with the Sustainable Value Foundation

ISLAND PRESS is a trademark of The Center for Resource Economics.

Library of Congress Cataloging-in-Publication Data.

The Library of Congress has cataloged the hardcover edition as follows:
Laszlo, Christopher.
  The sustainable company : how to create lasting value through social and environmental performance / Chris Laszlo.
    p. cm.
Includes bibliographical references and index.
ISBN 1-55963-836-2 (cloth : alk. paper)
1. Industrial management. 2. Business ethics. 3. Industrial management—Environmental aspects. 4. Social responsibility of business. 5. Industrial management—Case studies. I. Title.
  HD31.L31568 2003
  658.4'08—dc21
                                        2003011301
ISBN 1-59726-018-5 (pbk.: alk. paper)

British Cataloguing-in-Publication data available.

Printed on recycled, acid-free paper

Manufactured in the United States of America

10 9 8 7 6 5 4 3 2 1

TO MY DAUGHTERS JENNA AND ISHANA

CONTENTS

FOREWORD

In August 2002, the Johannesburg World Summit on Sustainable Development celebrated the tenth anniversary of the Rio conference. A number of heads of state attended, but after the United States refused to ratify the Kyoto Protocol—and after the events of September 11, 2001, with the threat of terrorism and the difficult issues of poverty and war in so many places—few expected much from the intergovernmental conference. It may have come as a surprise to some observers, but business was more present and more forceful in its determination to push ahead. One of the highlights of the gathering was an unlikely joint declaration by Greenpeace and the World Business Council for Sustainable Development (WBCSD), an organization of more than 100 international companies, about the need for coordinated international action against global warming.

The skeptics will say—and have said—that it was all marketing and communication. Companies, admittedly, do know how to use communication tools to their advantage. But I believe that real change is taking place. Unlike governments, large international companies have been following a steady course, recognizing more and more the strategic importance of sustainability in the world's future and in their own futures. After reading Chris Laszlo's book, one will understand better the depth and significance of this change of attitude.

Companies that depend greatly on natural resources—including energy—for the development of their business, such as Lafarge in the building materials industry, had never shared the pessimism of the Club of Rome doomsayers. They tend to believe strongly that technological progress can stretch the limits of possible performance, provided it is harnessed in the right direction. But they know that long-term efforts cannot always be spurred by short-term market signals, that a global conceptual framework is needed for long-term progress, and that recognizing issues and problems is the first step toward finding solutions.

So, for them, the concept of sustainable development, which looks at the long-term consequences of our current actions, is naturally attractive. Looking ahead for ways to conserve natural resources, mitigate global warming, or contribute to social development is the best way to avoid surprises and crises, inevitably followed by emergencies and emotional reactions, most of which are likely to have enormous economic costs and consequences.

The forward-looking international company is not concerned only about the long-term environmental future of the planet. It is working in an increasingly global marketplace, but one in which hostile feelings have sometimes developed. This global world is still a place where violence, poverty, inequality, prejudice, illiteracy, and racial and religious hatred exist. Many people see international companies as the villains, who not only benefit from, but also sometimes even contribute to, these ills. On the contrary, many international companies know that we cannot solve the world's problems, but we also know that we are contributing a positive influence. We bring jobs, increased standards of living, education, and training. We bring together people from different backgrounds and different origins, allowing them to communicate, to travel, to learn about each other; and we bring the world a little bit closer to the "global village" advertised too early. Our positive contributions must be recognized if we want to continue to be free to develop and if a market economy is to remain widely accepted.

For a company to commit to sustainable development makes good business sense. An approach that pays attention to all of a firm's stakeholders, however, will appear to some to be a deviation from the only worthwhile and legitimate objective of a company: the maximization of shareholder value. This book will show them that there need not be any contradiction between the two objectives. Actually, after the end of the 2000–2001 period, when the myths of instantaneous and limitless value creation often led to greedy and unethical behavior, it should not be difficult to recognize that real sustainable value creation for shareholders also requires attention to a company's other stakeholders.

The most encouraging development in favor of the sustainable company has been the behavior of the shareholders themselves. Business executives were sometimes worried to see a large part of the financial world adopting a narrow and myopic view of business and management objectives. It comforts them to observe the recent growth of "ethical funds" for shareholders who want to invest only in companies that will respect sustainable development criteria.

This is precisely where long-term self-interest and moral imperatives converge. Here managers and shareholders, who are also people with a conscience, can together shape a new business environment and, to quote Davos's motto, "contribute to a better world."

Bertrand Collomb
Chairman and CEO, Lafarge S.A.
January 2003

FOREWORD

Some may find my message surprising, but I observe that many leading corporations are no longer seeing environmental stewardship (or responsibilities to stakeholders other than shareholders) as a cost—a necessary evil, if you will. They are seeing these responsibilities as opportunities, a potential source of competitive advantage. Although this is not yet true for the vast majority of smaller firms, to the extent that leading companies change and set the terms of engagement and proactively address their social impacts to reduce costs and risks, win customers, and build reputation, the smaller firms will have to follow in order to stay in the game.

This is a change in view, even for the leaders. I must stress, however, that this change is based on self-interest, not altruism, and this fact is good not only for shareholders but also for the environment and those who care about it. If corporate efforts are born of self-interest, they are more real and sustainable and less susceptible to the business cycle. This change in orientation may be coming in the nick of time, or maybe it is just that the times are demanding the change.

The key challenge of our time is to provide the economic growth needed by the world's poor while leaving the local, regional, and global environment in a state that will provide sustenance and benefits in the future. The signs of stress in this equation are all around us. The economic needs are clear: those living in abject poverty number in the billions, and their number is likely to double over the next 50 years unless there is change. This poverty threatens everyone. Its symptoms include congestion, unemployment, undereducation, despair, unrest, terrorism, and disease. The disparity between rich and poor is evidence of this problem. The richest 15 percent consumes 75 percent of the world's resources, and the average American consumes 300 times the amount consumed by those at the other end of the economic scale. The gap is growing, and so is the aspiration for greater equity. So the alleviation of poverty on a massive scale is absolutely necessary.

Can our natural systems support the economic growth that will be necessary to lift up the growing numbers of poor? Our stocks of renewable resources (such as fish, forests, water, and soil) are falling. Waste accumulations (CO_2 and toxics) are rising. Biodiversity is being lost as humans sequester a greater share of the earth's photosynthesis. To bring the current world population to a Western standard of living would require material flow to increase 20 times.

Can our natural world handle this? Some would say it is doubtful. Nevertheless, can we deny the world's poor a decent way of life and some sense of equity? Not if we are to live in a safe and free world!

Leading corporations such as BP, Shell, Dupont, Honda, GM, and many others see these overwhelming forces gathering and are drawing the following conclusions:

- Action is required to preserve (and extend) open societies and markets that might be threatened by precipitous and calamitous environmental change.
- Opportunities to help abound, in the form of new technologies that raise living standards while reducing the human footprint.
- The private sector is well positioned with skills and the flexibility to answer the greatest needs.

Leading corporations see that change is coming and want to be sure they shape that change to their advantage. Therefore, they are going "beyond compliance" to seek out competitive advantage in the shaping of markets, the creation of new products and services, the formation of the right alliances, and the learning of the best practices for the new world that is coming.

The best example I have of this type of corporate behavior is what BP has done relative to the issue of global climate change. In the late 1990s, the global oil industry was in nearly complete denial of the importance of this issue. Climate change and its relationship to the use of fossil fuels called into question the basic value of this business to society. Nevertheless, BP broke ranks and began to address the issue head-on. It entered the policy debate; it announced emissions reductions in advance of any regulation; it began to learn about the future by instituting its own carbon trading scheme in partnership with Environmental Defense, sponsoring studies of future technology paths and joining rainforest protection schemes; and it pushed aggressively into the renewable energy realm through its photovoltaic business. It also started working in partnership with the auto companies on fuel-cell research that might eventually replace the internal combustion engine and its need for petroleum.

You might ask why BP would take such a radical and visible stance, given the potential loss of so much in its core business. BP is a big and complex company, and there are never simple answers to such questions. But it is clear to me that what many people saw as BP doing the "right thing" was actually a reflection of self-interest, and I believe that this has led to many good things for BP, including a newly defined and differentiated vision of its future captured in the term "Beyond Petroleum." Because the business case has become real, I believe that BP's efforts will be sustained, and that can only be good for the planet and the sustainability challenges we face.

There are many other examples of corporate transformation based on the ideas of sustainability and responsibility, and the list grows daily. The message of this book is that corporate responsibility is needed and corporations will be rewarded for providing it.

Richard Whately once said, "A man is called selfish, not for pursing his own good, but for neglecting his neighbor's." By that definition, corporations would be foolish to be selfish—because they would be missing so many good opportunities.

Steve Percy
Former Chairman and CEO, BP Americas
May 2003

Since this book first appeared in 2003, the challenge to integrate sustainability into the core businesses of companies has continued to grow. CEOs of leading global corporations are increasingly taking on environmental and social challenges, not as a fringe project delegated to sustainability specialists, but as a central business strategy. Companies in industries as diverse as insurance (for example, AVIVA Plc.) and automobiles (for example, Toyota) are making important strides in generating financial value from their sustainability performance.

To take just one example of recent developments, the business case is now much stronger for the hybrid cars described in Chapter 10. The book's original edition mentions 36,000 hybrid vehicles sold by Toyota between 1997 and 2002; the company's second-generation hybrid Prius sold 100,000 units in 2004 alone, with a six-month waiting list in markets such as the U.S. Clearly the number of consumers who want to drive cars with radically increased fuel economy and lower emissions outstripped even Toyota's best-case expectations.

Leading business schools have begun offering Executive Education programs that emphasize business competitiveness as the driving theme. Until recently, only a few specialized sustainability programs existed for executives and these were focused on the moral responsibility of corporations to make the world a better place rather than on value creation. At INSEAD, a leading European business school, over a thousand executives have used this book in the CEDEP Executive Education and Advanced Management Seminars as part of their participation in general management programs. Improving a company's sustainability performance is increasingly seen simply as a smart business decision.

Unfortunately, it is still too often the case that executives and line managers who have profit and loss responsibility are confused about what sustainability means for them. They hear conflicting messages such as focus on short-term shareholder value *or* focus on good corporate citizenship. They are unclear as to whether sustainability is an ethical constraint, a corporate public-relations effort, a regulatory compliance initiative, philanthropy, or a real change to how they should run their businesses.

This book, along with many other excellent works in the field, is designed to help readers understand what sustainability is, why it is important for business advantage, and how business managers can begin to incorporate environmental and social performance in their own organizations. Like every author I hope my book will continue to be widely read. In addition, I hope its key messages will resonate with practitioners in a way that leads to changes in how business is conducted.

The Problem and the Challenge

There is a growing rift between short-term profit thinking in companies and social and environmental pressures from stakeholders. Globalization, ecological stresses, and terrorism are all facets of a new, more complex reality featuring multiple stakeholders and new corporate responsibilities. Yet business executives often view corporate responsibility as adding complexity and cost in an economic environment that can ill afford them. Inside corporations, financial executives don't understand the roles of environment, health, and safety managers. Social and environmental goals are almost always developed apart from business strategy: different terminologies, different departments and managers, different measures, and different reporting tools. The triple bottom line is often exactly that: three distinct sets of performance measures. Now the challenge is to go beyond the triple bottom line to find a new, more integrated approach to measuring and managing business performance.

The Book's Three-Part Structure

In Part I, many of the key sustainability concepts are presented through the eyes of a CEO from the 1960s through today (Chapter 1). This is followed by a look at the rise of stakeholder consciousness and planetary ethics (Chapter 2), discussions of how sustainable value creation is measured and benchmarked (Chapters 3 and 4), and an explanation of the mind-set and organizational culture required for transformation (Chapter 5).

Part II provides case studies of leading responsible companies that demonstrate, to varying degrees, how sustainability can make good business sense. At either the project level, or the company-wide level, these leading companies have enriched their shareholders by exceeding compliance standards for environmental and social performance. Their struggles and failures provide lessons as important as any of the successes usually trumpeted in the media. In each case, the reader has an opportunity to see sustainable value creation in action.

Part III offers a tool kit for managers who want to know how they can transform their organizations to create sustainable value for their shareholders and stakeholders. It gives a step-by-step approach to developing sustainable value strategies and helps readers identify how and where they can create that value. The frameworks and tools provide the practitioner with the resources to design business strategies for the twenty-first century.

Great Falls, VA
June 2005

ACKNOWLEDGMENTS

The material for this book was researched in collaboration with current and former executives at Lafarge, Patagonia, Bulmers, Procter & Gamble, Celanese, Polaroid, The Co-operative Bank, Dupont, General Motors, Hewlett-Packard, Anheuser-Busch, Intel, Dow Chemical, Air Transat, Solvay, Exelon, and many other companies. My colleagues Dave Sherman and John Whalen at Sustainable Value Partners, Inc., were instrumental in developing and testing many of the tools and frameworks presented in Part III. They bring a wealth of management experience and process skills to the practical aspects of moving organizations to sustainable value creation.

Other colleagues and friends to whom I owe a debt of thanks include Jib Ellison, John Buffington, Mark Major, Joseph Rinkevich, Enrico Bauer, Dan Sayre, Jean-François Laugel, Frank Loy, Dr. Herbert Fockler, Dr. Craig Schiffries, Darryl Banks, Bob Faron, Mino Akhtar, Adam Pattantyus, Susan Svoboda, Gary Fuhrman, Tom Davis, Sandra Waddock, Ira Feldman, Ned Hulbert, Yasuhiko Kimura, Laara Lindo, Dr. Ann Goodman, Dom Fielden, Suzanne Fielden, Don Carli, Jan Kristof, and Don Hawley. The work was further developed in a course I give four times a year in the executive program at INSEAD-CEDEP in France, on the subject of creating shareholder value through corporate responsibility. A special word of thanks to Dr. Alexander Laszlo and Dr. Kathia Castro Laszlo, for their work on evolutionary development.

The research also benefited from the work of a handful of sustainability benchmarking and reporting organizations pursuing similar objectives, among which the following must be acknowledged for their path-breaking work: the World Business Council for Sustainable Development (WBCSD), the World Resources Institute (WRI), the Global Environmental Management Initiative (GEMI), the Caux Roundtable, the Coalition for Environmentally Responsible Economies (CERES), and the Global Reporting Initiative. The search for performance metrics, particularly nonfinancial indicators that measure the quality of stakeholder relations, benefited from my partnership with several socially responsible investment rating agencies around the world: in the United States, INNOVEST Strategic Value Advisors (Dr. Matthew Kiernan, Hewson Baltzell, Frank Dixon, Peter Wilkes, Pierre Trevet), the Total Social Impact Foundation (Steve Dillenburg, CFA, and Tim Greene, Ph.D.); in the UK and France, Core Ratings (Alan Banks, Geneviève Ferone); in Australia, the Sustainable Investment Research Institute (Mark Bytheway); in Brazil, UNIBANCO (Christopher Wells) and Atitude (Fernando Salgado, Cristiana Improta, and Cibele Salviatto).

A major influence in shaping the core message of this book has been the author's father, Ervin Laszlo, a visionary scientist, futurist, and author of over 60 books, who has dedicated much of his life to raising awareness of the need for global stakeholder responsibility. He was among the first to refer to this whole-systems responsibility as planetary ethics. In 1993, he founded the Club of Budapest, an association of world-renowned leaders dedicated to promoting planetary ethics in every field of human endeavor. Its members include the Dalai Lama, Vaclav Havel, Mikhail Gorbachev, Desmond Tutu, Peter Ustinov, Peter Gabriel, and young and creative people in many parts of the world. Their work has helped to articulate a new way of thinking and a new way of living based on the challenges and constraints of an increasingly fragile planet. The business implications of planetary ethics contribute to a compelling motive for stakeholder satisfaction, based on the idea that if business does not begin to take responsibility for its impacts on society and nature, there will soon be neither left for it.

My agent Danielle Jatlow of Waterside Productions, Inc., promoted the book's message with tireless enthusiasm, and Bill Gladstone, president and founder of Waterside Productions, Inc., provided visionary inspiration at key moments in the writing process. Todd Baldwin at Island Press is a senior editor whose standards of excellence and vision for the book were all that an author could wish for. To Todd and the entire Island Press team, I express my heartfelt thanks.

A Business Case Approach

As suggested in these acknowledgments, the book was born of two separate but converging logics—one market-based and one ethical. Together they make a compelling business case for corporate responsibility as executives seek to respond to market opportunities and transform their organizations in pursuit of a more sustainable world. This approach explicitly avoids the dilemma commonly posed by social activists who force executives to choose between being responsible (moral goals) and being profitable (business goals). Sustainable value is created from the shared interests of stakeholders and shareholders. As you read about the stakeholder dimension it is useful to see it through the lens of emerging key success factors for business. It doesn't require the reader to be convinced of a particular moral or political point of view; in fact, it really doesn't matter if the reader believes in the existence of a new ethics at all. Creating stakeholder value, and linking that value to the wealth-creating capacity of the company, is the practical business challenge that lies at the heart of this book.

The book's message—and the wager of the visionary corporate leaders shown in the four case studies—is that an integrated economic, social, and environmental approach leads to more enduring shareholder value than a short-term profit approach that transfers value from one or more stakeholders to the company's shareholders. It is a long-term strategy, uniquely relevant to the twenty-first century, in which responsible social change can become a source of innovation and profit rather than an added cost.

PART I

The Leap to Sustainable Value

INTRODUCTION

Hᴵᴳʜ-ᴘʀᴏꜰɪʟᴇ ᴄᴏʀᴘᴏʀᴀᴛᴇ ꜱᴄᴀɴᴅᴀʟꜱ such as Philip Morris, Bridgestone/Firestone, the *Exxon Valdez,* Union Carbide in Bhopal, Rio Tinto at Freeport, Shell at Brent Spar, Nike's shoe factories in Vietnam, Archer Daniel Midland's indictment on 2,300 counts of price fixing—and, most recently, Enron, Vivendi, Arthur Anderson, Global Crossings, Merrill Lynch, Tyco, and WorldCom—have raised market awareness of corporate responsibility. So has the bankruptcy of K-Mart, rated last of the Standard and Poor 500 (S&P 500) companies in 2001 in terms of corporate responsibility by a leading U.S. ethical investment ratings agency. In the first quarter of 2002, the U.S. Securities and Exchange Commission (SEC) opened 64 financial reporting cases—more than twice the number in the 2001 first quarter—as part of its crackdown on corporate crime, targeting such large well-known companies as Arthur Anderson (also under federal indictment), Computer Associates, Qwest, and Xerox, among others.

These dramatic cases are generally recognized to be only the tip of the iceberg. They are not the whole story, and they do not reflect the business benefits and sources of value creation presented in this book. Moreover, the crisis of corporate responsibility in the developed world overlooks the tremendous benefits that could be gained in the developing world simply from improving the lot of 4 billion people currently living on the margins of the global market system (see, for example, C. K. Prahalad and Stuart Hart's "The Fortune at the Bottom of the

Pyramid"). George Carpenter, the head of Procter & Gamble's (P&G's) corporate sustainability department, recently stated that his goal is now $1 billion in additional revenues from "sustainability" products and services. P&G already has such products aimed at "doing well and doing good" in the developing world, ranging from Actonel® (reduces the risk of hip fracture in elderly women with osteoporosis) to Nutra Star® (a nutritional drink that provides Vitamin A, iodine, and iron). The company is investing to bring clean drinking water to Sub-Saharan Africa. Why? Because so many of its products require clean drinking water, and until African villages have it, P&G's market on that continent will be limited.

A growing segment of consumers, investors, employees, communities and nongovernmental organizations (NGOs) are defining what constitutes sustainable business conduct and demanding such conduct. These constituents are collectively developing a new class of sustainability performance indicators. In effect, companies are finding that sustainability performance is a source of differentiation that helps to create (or destroy) shareholder value and to manage risks.

In the past, a combination of environmental experts armed with technical scientific knowledge, legal experts representing regulatory requirements, and political parties forced executives to adopt more ethical business practices. Internal values and principles reflecting top management's personal commitment to bettering society were another influence for greater stakeholder responsibility. Only since 1995 has a market-driven "logic of sustainability" emerged based on meeting expectations of stakeholder performance. The "five logics of sustainability" shown below make a compelling case for a more *mainstream* transformation from short-term profit focus to stakeholder management.

1. Scientific, such as evidence of human-induced global climate change
2. Regulatory, such as title I of the Clean Air Act (amended 1990) in the United States
3. Political, such as the Green Parties' agenda in Europe

4. Moral, based on values and principles
5. Market, focusing on the shareholder value implications of stake-holder value

These five logics are converging into a coherent story that business ignores at its peril. In a strongly interacting and highly interdependent global economic system, the interests of the shareholders are increasingly coinciding with the interests of society and the environment.

In this book, we will touch on all five drivers of stakeholder management while giving particular attention to the fifth category: the market drivers of sustainability. This emphasis reflects the belief that to engage the business community, we need to do so on its own terms: we need to make a business case for it.

The ethical argument for stakeholder management extends well beyond religious or abstract moral principles. Globalization is giving rise to a "naturalistic" ethics based on the fact that the health and well-being of business, society, and nature have become inextricably entwined. As Ryuzaburo Kabu, honorary chairman of Canon, Inc., said,

> Global corporations rely on educated workers, consumers with money to spend, a healthy natural environment, and peaceful existence between nations and ethnic groups. . . . At this watershed period in history, it is in the interests of the world's most powerful corporations to work for the advancement of global peace and prosperity. To put it simply, global companies have no future if the earth has no future.

If companies are to make the evolutionary leap in business purpose that globalization is calling for, they need to replace an exclusive focus on shareholders with a strategy in which stakeholder value is pursued as a part of the core business purpose. Stakeholder strategy takes into account the impact and consequences of a company's operations on everyone who is affected by them. Dr. Deborah Anderson, president of Farsight Associates Inc. and former vice president for environmental quality worldwide at Procter & Gamble, defines stakeholders as anyone who can help or hurt a business. By this definition, stakeholders include not just shareholders but also customers, employees, and business partners; local communities; government; worldwide public opinion; NGOs; and activists who represent the natural environment.

Throughout this book, the terms *corporate responsibility* and *sustainability* are used interchangeably. To some extent, this usage reflects the lack of consensus about what these terms mean in the business world. Some executives prefer the term corporate responsibility and consider sustainability to be a vague and ill-defined concept, whereas others prefer the opposite. For both terms as used in the book, the central idea is caring for stakeholders and assessing the impact of products, services, and the conduct of companies on the well-being of these stakeholders.

In 1987, at a groundbreaking symposium of international governments, the World Commission on Environment and Development (the so-called Brundtland Commission) was the first to define sustainability: "the ability to meet today's global economic, environmental and social needs without compromising the opportunity for future generations to meet theirs." This definition continues to be widely used today. The Dow Jones Sustainability Group Index (DJSGI) gives another useful definition: "a business approach to creating long-term shareholder value by embracing opportunities and risks deriving from economic, environmental, and social developments." The "New Ethics in Business" (Chapter 2) includes additional definitions, as well as a discussion of the mind-set, behaviors, and practices associated with sustainable value.

Extending consideration to stakeholders is not a charitable adjunct to a successful business strategy but an intrinsic element of it. Integrating economic, social, and environmental objectives into a single bottom line can be a significant source of innovation and top-line growth. Companies that make the transition from focusing exclusively on shareholders to managing for stakeholder satisfaction will survive consolidation and attrition in today's marketplace and become leading actors in the global world of the twenty-first century.

It will become evident to the reader early on that sustainability leadership is not coming primarily from the Global 100 companies: the Exxon Mobils, Wal-Marts, and General Electrics. The world's largest public companies are perhaps under too much pressure from the capital markets, and those that heavily adopt the practice of granting stock options to their senior executives are further reinforcing the logic of near-term profitability. Many of the large, publicly held companies might also fear that they will open themselves to stockholder lawsuits (even if unmerited) if they try to pioneer the sustainability route.

Instead, sustainability leadership is coming from a growing number of companies with sales ranging from $100 million to $2 billion, often ones with private or semiprivate ownership (or recently reverted to private ownership, such as Levi-Strauss). Such companies often show a strong founder's influence and are looking for a unique source of differentiation to escape the technology innovation rat race that their bigger competitors are increasingly likely to win. Living their values and branding their identity in terms of social and environmental responsibility is becoming a way to survive in the marketplace. Two of the companies discussed in this book—Patagonia and The Co-operative Bank—are examples of this strategic differentiation. Bulmers is listed on the London Stock Exchange but has just over half its ownership under family control. Atlantic Richfield Corporation was acquired by BP Amoco in 2000.

These sustainability leaders, and others like them around the world, are pursuing a vision for betterment that is also in their self-interest. In doing so, they are returning business to its role as "builder of civilizations," as envisioned by corporate chieftains such as IBM's Thomas J. Watson, Sr., at the beginning of the twentieth century. This book is aimed at the corporate chieftains of the new century.

CHAPTER ONE

Toward an
Integrated Bottom Line

IN 1963, a young and newly appointed chief executive officer (CEO), Michael Watts, is reflecting on the mission and purpose of his business. From the executive suite, he looks out into the courtyard of his company's main production facility and sees an orderly scheduling of work. Employees are arriving at an early hour and fulfilling their daily jobs in specialized roles. Suppliers deliver parts and settle invoices with scant further contact with the company's employees. Retail customers have no contact at all with this facility—they order monthly from the company's salesmen, based on projected retail inventories that reflect consumer preferences that Michael Watts knows only from occasional focus groups. The entire company is organized around four functions: general management, production, sales, and finance.

Michael's main focus is financial results. He regularly tracks returns on invested capital, operating profit, debt issuance, and projected dividends to the company's shareholders. Luckily for him, his departments are highly autonomous and keep all the activity going efficiently with a minimum of intervention—for the moment. Innovations in technology, competitor pressures, and profound shifts in consumer values and preferences will soon force the company to make major changes.

Fast-forward 30 years to 1993. Much of the company's effort has been spent tearing down the walls between departments and functions. Computer integrated manufacturing (CIM) and integrated software platforms connect each production facility to its customers and ultimately to the consumer in real time. Operational measures of customer satisfaction, internal processes, and the organization's innovative activities complement financial measures. A balanced scorecard offers all executives a fast but comprehensive view of the business.

Still 10 years away from retirement, Michael now feels a deep satisfaction at having built an integrated value chain. No one can speak about the existence of "silos" in his organization. His one source of concern is a manufacturing safety function renamed, in the late 1980s, environment, health, and safety (EH&S). A former site engineer with a legal background now heads it, yet Michael simply can't seem to settle this function into his management team. Waste-permitting, site remediation, resource depletion targets, pollution prevention, and environmental product design parameters are things that his business unit heads don't want to hear about. As long as the company is complying with government regulations, EH&S would serve the team best by sticking to its legal and technical area of expertise.

Then one morning Susan Aldrin, Michael's chosen successor, walks into his office and begins talking about the need for the company's environmental policies to become more integrated into business operations. Susan speaks of the need to be proactive on safety measures in the plant and to reduce workplace accidents to zero through better training and new safe manufacturing processes. She outlines a plan for implementing an Environmental Management System (EMS) that would help the company move toward closed-loop production, reducing waste and pollution. "I want each business unit to track the full impact of its activities on the environment," says Susan. A few days later, Michael talks to his EH&S manager, who responds enthusiastically to what they both agree is an opportunity to begin "tearing down the Green Wall": removing the great divide between environmental performance and business performance. Business managers need to see environmental managers as equals and work together better on shared objectives. A new campaign begins to integrate strategic environmental management into the business, and in the process EH&S is invited to the table as a full partner.

With only a year to go before retirement, Michael is pleased to learn that his company has been awarded a prize for environmental excellence.

His managers regularly speak about the double bottom line and, increasingly, about the triple bottom line. A United Way campaign reaches a statewide high for employee participation, and a patronage-of-the-arts program earns the company additional prestige. Although it is costing his company 0.5 percent of profits, the sense of satisfaction derived from contributing to society is evident and is shared within the executive group.

Then one morning, the CEO's phone rings on his private line. It is his daughter, Gretchen, who is calling from Port-au-Prince; she and her husband have decided to adopt a little Haitian girl and urgently need him to come to Haiti to help convince the local authorities to file for expedited adoption. He departs that afternoon, leaving Susan in charge, with the admonition to "make sure everyone understands what we need to do to meet next quarter's Earnings-per-share (EPS) targets."

Arriving in Port-au-Prince, Michael's plane emerges from a cloud bank to reveal a vista of shantytowns, poverty, dirt, and overcrowding the likes of which he has never seen before. A feeling of repulsion is replaced with a desire to use his executive skills to resolve the adoption situation in his daughter's favor. At the Ministry of the Interior, he soon finds himself signing papers, giving officials "dash" where needed to expedite the process, and no longer feeling concerned about his unpleasant surroundings. That evening he checks into a hotel, ready to complete formalities the next day and return home. This turns out to be far less simple than he could ever have imagined.

The following morning, he and Gretchen take a taxi 50 miles west of the capital to the shantytown of Fond Verrettes. A ministry official takes them to the local adoption center, where Michael comes face to face with one of his own company's chemical suppliers. A local guide points to the cloudy brownish water coming from the town's fountain and describes how toxic runoff from this supplier's facility has poisoned the town's drinking water. Impoverished farmers had moved their families close to the factory in the hope of earning a meager wage of $1 a day. In the course of their work, they often stand barefoot for hours at a time in vats polluted with chemical residue, and they now suffer from a range of respiratory ailments and skin conditions. No school or hospital exists in this town, nor have the foreign-owned factories offered to contribute to building any.

Across the street, Michael's practiced eye sees obvious signs that his company's chemical supplier has no health and safety plan for its employees. Most of the manual workers here are exhausted, and some appear deprived of basic dignities. A supervisor appears to strike a woman who is visibly slowing down in unpacking a truck container of 50-kilogram bags. The youngest workers here are no more than about 12 years old.

The air is thick with fumes—Michael recognizes the telltale signs of SO_x and NO_x emissions. A quick look westward tells Michael that the richly biodiverse forests in this part of Haiti have been razed to make way for storage depots and truck repair shops. The scene is desolate indeed.

Three hours after his arrival in Fond Verrettes, Michael's newly adopted granddaughter runs smiling into his arms. With tears in his eyes, Michael begins to comprehend the difference between what is important and what is essential in his life. Making money, succeeding in business, and winning are important. His daughter and grand-daughter and their future well-being are essential. In that moment of clarity, Michael begins to see that he and his company do lots of good but also do some unintentional damage—for example, allowing suppliers to treat employees and local communities badly, ignoring human rights violations in some countries, and disregarding the impact of wastes on the environment. There are many other harmful aspects of his business that he has been overlooking uncomfortably for some time. Michael had recently been hearing about emerging ethics standards for business conduct. He knows that his company is increasingly evaluated on its social and environmental performance. What now crystallizes for Michael is the *possibility* of succeeding in business without doing harm to the company's stakeholders around the world.

That afternoon, Michael makes a silent commitment to modify his company's mission to include better care for people and for the flora, fauna, and living systems that made up the planet. And he resolves to do this without sacrificing business performance—in fact, he envisions succeeding better than ever before.

When he returns to work the following Monday, Michael calls an executive committee meeting and shares his vision of an integrated sustainability strategy. Henceforth the primary purpose of the business will be to create value for shareholders and stakeholders together, in what Michael refers to as *sustainable value*—in other words, lasting value based on economic, social, and environmental performance. It will now be unacceptable for any business unit manager not to know the impact of his or her unit on a broad set of stakeholders, including employees, local communities, and nature. It will be unacceptable to create shareholder value by transferring a portion of that value from another stakeholder group. The heart of the issue, Michael tells his team, is that this is a business proposition. If we continue to operate in Haiti the way we have, we will incur growing liabilities with the people, with the government, and with watchdog groups representing the environment of that country. Such conduct represents a business risk that no longer makes sense in today's world of instant and transparent reporting, emerging green consumers, and socially responsible investors.

His team has never heard him speak like this before. With heart and spirit, he shares his commitment to have the company succeed economically while bettering the lot of all its stakeholders. As a starting point, he organizes staggered trips for every employee to visit at least one of the company's sourcing sites in the developing world. Afterward, there are in-house retreats to reflect on the future course of the business.

At this point, a detailed analysis of value creation begins. Stakeholder value and impact are assessed along with traditional sources of shareholder value. The strategic planning processes in both the business units and the financial accounts gradually integrate stakeholder value and impact along the entire value chain. Exactly how business value is created from social and environmental responsibility is made clear to each key operations manager. A new era begins in which the company seeks competitive advantage not just *in* the world but *for* the world.

Three years later, under Susan Aldrin's leadership, the company has a vendor code of conduct with all 800 of its suppliers, along with training and development programs to help them adhere to it. Guidelines are developed to assess and determine action for ethical violations, particularly in poorer developing countries. Business unit heads find that it is good business practice to offer preferential status to suppliers who respect universal ethical standards by treating people with dignity. Supplier loyalty is up and turnover down. By redesigning selected product lines to take into account life-cycle impacts, from raw materials to end-of-life product disposal, and by tracking resources used as well as outputs and environmental impacts, the company has come up with entirely new market offerings. This approach has allowed it to expand into underserved markets and grow its business overall. Innovation and ecoefficiency projects have reduced costs in unexpected ways, contributing to improved profit margins. Several NGOs have contributed technical knowledge to the innovation process. Best of all, a small core group of loyal consumers is beginning to buy the company's products simply because it is living up to environmental and social values. In a highly competitive market, this "sustainable value edge" is making a significant difference.

The journey from 1963 to the present tells a composite story that reflects the multiple realities companies experience as they transform their value delivery to embrace social and environmental responsibility. This book profiles some of the companies from which this composite is drawn. Transformations driven by visionary leaders such as Yvon Chouinard and Michael Crooke (Patagonia) and Ray Anderson (Interface) and the company-wide strategies of Toyota, Lafarge, Shell, and The Co-operative Bank are becoming part of the new business landscape.

The pattern is increasingly clear. Michael Watts began his role as CEO at a time when the company's focus was exclusively on economic results and its departments operated without much interaction with one another (the bottom left square of Figure 1-1). In the decades that followed, the company moved to a more integrated value chain by introducing new processes to improve quality, reduce defects, and raise customer satisfaction. In the 1990s, the company began integrating

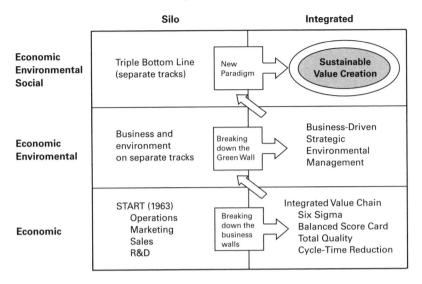

Figure 1-1. The CEO's Journey

environmental performance into business performance ("breaking down the Green Wall"). Social performance targets were added in 2000.

Until the CEO's epiphany brought about by his personal journey, the company's journey was about incremental change. The final step (from the top left square to the top right square in Figure 1-1) to a sustainable value strategy represents a paradigm shift. This theme of transformation, explored further in Chapter 5, is one of the core messages of the book. Corporations as an institution are facing the prospect of an evolutionary leap to sustainable value—or irrelevance and extinction. Making this leap successfully will require both a shift in mind-set and practical initiatives integrated into operations.

CHAPTER TWO

The New Ethics
in Business

THE EMERGENCE of a new ethics in business is rapidly changing what we mean by the term *corporate responsibility*. The new ethics is market-driven but values-based. It originates with changing social expectations as expressed by consumers, employees, investors, business partners, local communities, and environmental activists. It is not political in the sense of attempting to impose the beliefs of one group on another group; it is not moralistic because it does not exhort companies to adopt one or another moral ideology. By market-driven, we mean that the underlying logic is "if you want your business to succeed, here is a new set of measurable performance standards you have to meet."

We call the new ethics "planetary" because it expands the code of business conduct to the globe. It encompasses a company's responsibility for society and the environment, and it shifts the moral basis of action from abstract questions of right and wrong (such as "don't lie to your boss") to a consideration of whether a company is operating sustainably. Businesses now face a constellation of interests: market, social, and environmental. These interests call for companies to integrate stakeholder objectives as part of the way they do business.

In this sense, the new ethics can be thought of as a dynamic standard for pursuing profitability that allows future generations an equal opportunity to do so. It echoes the Brundtland Commission's definition of sustainability: "the ability to meet today's global economic, environmental and social needs without compromising the opportunity for future generations to meet theirs."

Planetary ethics calls for operating within the earth's social and physical limits (hence its name). Although science and technology continually redefine these limits, the fact is that we no longer operate in a world where human growth and the physical capacities of nature appear endless and unbounded. "Throughout history," says author Ross Gelbspan, "it has been philosophers, religious leaders, and revolutionaries who have asked us to reexamine our values, our relationships, our purposes, and the way we live. Now we are being asked by the oceans."[1]

To the distress of those who advocate unbounded consumerism, planetary ethics will likely involve restraint, particularly in countries such as the United States, where the per capita use of resources would require several planet earths if everyone in the world chose to live at U.S. standards. Gandhi once said, "Live simply so that others may simply live." With a growing world population of 6 billion, the ecological stress of everyone's trying to achieve the material lifestyle of America quickly becomes untenable.

But as William McDonough and Michael Braungart point out in their best-seller, *Cradle-to-Cradle*, reducing the impact of our species is not only about making do with less. It is also about redesigning our products and processes so that human industry becomes a source of nourishment rather than waste. McDonough and Braungart vividly contrast the old design paradigm with the new one. Here is how they describe the existing industrial system:[2]

- Puts billions of pounds of toxic material into the air, water, and soil every year
- Produces some materials so dangerous they will require constant vigilance by future generations
- Results in gigantic amounts of waste
- Puts valuable materials in holes all over the planet, where they can never be retrieved
- Requires thousands of complex regulations to keep people and natural systems from being poisoned too quickly

- Measures productivity by how few people are working
- Creates prosperity by digging up or cutting down natural resources and then burying or burning them
- Erodes the diversity of species and cultural practices

When the current industrial design is stated in this way, it quickly becomes obvious that we cannot continue our business practices without courting disaster. A revolution in design is unlikely to result from technological innovation or market incentives alone.

Planetary ethics is not only about environmental sustainability. It is also about the social dimension—the fourth principle of The Natural Step (an international organization that uses a science-based, systems framework to help organizations and communities understand and move toward sustainability): "There must be a just and efficient use of energy and other resources." Planetary ethics, by its nature, is indivisible: a company cannot be responsible in its environmental practices and negligent in its community relations or social impacts. On the global level, we cannot conserve and restore nature while allowing billions of people to live at the edge of poverty and be excluded from the economic benefits of the global marketplace.

In this social context, it is interesting to consider the case of Wal-Mart, the world's largest retailer. Over the years, Wal-Mart has developed strong environmental practices and achieved renown for its ecostore in Lawrence, Kansas, with its center for environment education, one-stop recycling, low-energy building design, and use of sustainably harvested wood in its roof and ceiling structure. And yet does this make Wal-Mart a model of the new ethics? Not if you listen to David Norris of the nonprofit Institute for Local Self-Reliance:

> Wal-Mart's Kansas ecostore has received enormous publicity but the context for the store is egregious. Wal-Mart has done the same thing everywhere. It moves into an area, drives out small business, drives out diversity—in short, undermines community. The fact that the Wal-Mart operation in Lawrence is an ecostore doesn't undo any of that.[3]

In effect, Norris is saying that for Wal-Mart to be seen as a responsible company, it would need to address its social impacts as well as its environmental ones and also that addressing one area without the other still makes it unsustainable.

A new ethics is required, one that stems from caring about stakeholders in all essential dimensions. But let's be clear about what we mean by ethics. It is not about telling people how they should act or about blaming anyone for choosing a particular lifestyle. It is about offering a better understanding of the nature of business and its impacts now and in the future. It is about catalyzing awareness of social and environmental realities, such as global warming. When we learn that glaciers are sliding into the sea at a suddenly increased rate—including a 1,250-square-mile section of the 600-foot-thick Larsen B ice shelf that collapsed in only 35 days early in 2002—we begin to look differently at an industry that produces heat-trapping carbon. When we learn that just one degree of warming is causing glaciers to melt, tundras to thaw, infectious diseases to migrate, and changes to occur in the timing of the seasons, we feel a renewed urgency in developing non-carbon-emitting industrial processes. Our sense of humankind's place on earth shifts with the realization that we consume nearly half the planet's net primary production (NPP), defined as the sum of all photosynthetic production minus the energy required to maintain and support the plants that are doing the "manufacturing." By the middle of this century, our species alone may be consuming nearly 80 percent of the planet's NPP.

Nevertheless, the idea of a planetary ethics is one with which business executives are usually not comfortable. "The ethical dimension of sustainable development is inescapable," says Carl Frankel, "yet as a matter of course is disregarded in the sustainable business world, which for the most part remains focused on technical issues, and indeed is often dismissive of what it views as all that impractical, pointy-headed theorizing."[4] The word *ethics* conjures images of moral fundamentalist preaching of right and wrong, and hearing the stricture to "live simply" leads some to feel that the American way of life and its associated freedoms are at stake. Although it may be tempting to avoid the ethics conversation altogether—and focus simply on the shareholder value aspects of sustainability—the challenges we face require that we deeply reexamine the conduct of business on a global scale.

Planetary ethics is not so much a list of dos and don'ts as it is a worldview we can use as a guide for the conduct of business. For example, planetary ethics does not say that combustion engine vehicles cannot be sold or purchased in China; it does say that global automobile manufacturers operating from a perspective of planetary ethics will integrate into their business objectives technological solutions such as hybrid electric and hydrogen fuel cells that will allow cars to be sold sustainably in China. Such an automobile manufacturer would clearly understand that if every adult in China and other populous developing countries drove a combustion engine vehicle, the emissions impact on the environment would be totally unsustainable, just as it is proving to be in the developed world. Incidentally, cars are estimated to consume half the world's oil and create nearly one-fifth of its greenhouse gases (these numbers include the car manufacturing process).[5]

As stated earlier, the prospect of grappling with a new ethics is not one that most executives welcome. Yet the choice between adopting and not adopting planetary ethics may well turn out to be the difference between a transformation to true sustainability and merely incremental change that maintains the existing paradigm of short-term shareholder value at any cost. In Figure 2-1, the gap between change path (A) and change path (B) is shown as the planetary ethics factor. Without this ethics factor, the level of change we will achieve is likely to be insufficient to reach the critical transformation required.

With the recent advent of international reporting standards such as the Global Reporting Initiative (GRI) (2000, revised 2002), performance standards such as the Organization for Economic Cooperation and Development (OECD) Guidelines of Corporate Responsibility (2001) and the UN Global Compact (1999), and socially responsible investment ratings of stakeholder performance—INNOVEST, Core-Ratings, Sustainable Asset Management (SAM)—this vague notion of planetary ethics is becoming measured, tracked, and publicized. Planetary ethics is entering the global marketplace, not because business has suddenly adopted a conscience—it has always had one —but because there is a growing demand for values and principles of sustainability.

Planetary Ethics Based on Timeless Principles

The principles that underlie planetary ethics in business are universal and timeless. As the visionary Walter Russell said nearly 100 years ago, "Moral and ethical principles are unchangeable, but the forms of their practice are continually changing in accordance with man's unfolding comprehension." A century ago, ethics in business took the form of ennobling man through industrial expansion and technology. For example, Henry Ford sought to make it possible for every man to afford a family automobile. At that time, ecological limits to growth were not apparent. Social disparities were local rather than global. A planetary ethics based on goals for a sustainable biosphere would not have made

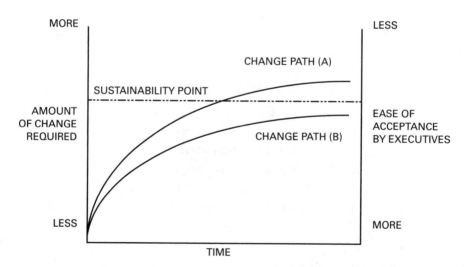

Figure 2-1. The New Ethics as a Key Enabler
Path (B) represents approaches to sustainability without a deep shift in awareness of stakeholders in a systems view of the world. Path (A) is only possible once individuals and organizations understand and adopt planetary ethics as a guide to business conduct.

sense then. And yet the fundamental moral aspirations of business leaders were the same as today. Thomas J. Watson, Sr., founder and chairman of IBM, delivered a series of lectures on business ethics in the 1920s and 1930s together with Walter Russell. What he said then is as relevant to planetary ethics today as it was to the industrial practices of his time.

> Great businesses must have the highest possible code of ethics. A balanced policy of honesty and fair dealings in business is not enough.... Business leaders are not just "doing business." They are knitting together the whole fabric of civilization. Its harmony, pattern, design, and mechanism are due to their clear thinking, ingenuity, progressiveness, imagination, and character. For this reason, business leaders must be equally interested and proficient in all of the elements which go to make up a civilization which is seeking to find peace, prosperity and happiness through united effort.[6]

Today, the principles of business have become planetary in form. They require accountability not only to our fellow human beings but also to the ecologies that support life on earth. Rights and obligations extend to shareholders, employees, and customers (as they already had to some extent by the 1920s) as well as to business partners, local communities, and the physical environment. As issues such as climate change make clear, our reach and impacts have become planetary in scale, and our vision and our commitments must expand to match them. The "unit of consciousness" is no longer one company or country but the whole planet.

Why a New Consciousness Is Needed

Despite the increasingly obvious imperative, few companies choose to exercise the new ethics. This is not because technological options are limited or marketplace opportunities and incentives are missing. The difficulty is in the mind-set that prevails in business. It is the consciousness of a planetary ethics—or the lack thereof—that poses the biggest challenge. Because many business leaders continue to operate from an antiquated view of business purpose, they are often tempted by superficial solutions to sustainability.

A business leader who views business activities only as producing a product or service for customers in order to maximize near-term profit will look at social and environmental performance as discretionary costs. Business leaders who take a narrow view of social and environmental obligations will be drawn to quick communication fixes, largely symbolic charters or purely technical compliance programs. They will use a nineteenth-century tool kit to solve twenty-first century problems, analyzing problems individually and engineering solutions based on maximizing short-term profits.

It is not that senior management, as a whole, is opposed to sustainability initiatives, either. They are usually (and understandably) focused on two things: what tangible results will be produced and what actions they need to take to get there. They may have an eye on their social and environmental context, but they simply don't have time to spend thinking about sustainability. If the case is there for achieving results, they would much rather just do it.

Sustainability represents a paradigm shift in business: it places corporations in a new role. Just as national institutions took on a new role in political governance after 1648, with a corresponding decline of the influence of the church and the nobility, so capitalism is reaching a watershed moment in history in which the purpose of the corporation— if it is to survive as an institution—will need to be transformed. Its new responsibilities correspond only to its newfound power. As Willis Harman has said, "Business has become, in this last half century, the most powerful institution on the planet. The dominant institution in any society needs to take responsibility for the whole—as the church did in the days of the Holy Roman Empire."[7]

What consumers, employees, and investors are demanding is a conduct of business that takes into account the effect of its activities on all its stakeholders. This requires creating a consciousness of greater connectedness with one another and with nature and an understanding of global problems that involves feeling and intuition as well as thinking.

The resulting mind-set will change planetary ethics from a blip on the corporate radar screen to a mainstream way of thinking and acting.

Planetary ethics represents a new design paradigm for business. In *Cradle-to-Cradle,* William McDonough and Michael Braungart begin to outline some of its features:

- Buildings that produce more energy than they consume, accrue and store solar energy, and purify their own waste water and release it slowly in a purer form
- Factory effluent water that is cleaner than the influent
- Products that, when their useful life is over, do not become useless waste but can be tossed onto the ground to decompose and become food for plants and animals, rebuilding soil; or, alternatively, can return to industrial cycles to supply high-quality raw materials for new products
- Billions, even trillions, of dollars' worth of materials accrued for human and natural purposes each year
- A world of abundance, not one of limits, pollution, and waste

Planetary Ethics or *Shareholder Value: Do We Have to Choose?*

Are executives being required to choose between ethics and shareholder value? Some would say that the answer to this question is yes: profit and ethics simply don't go together. Recent discussions about sustainability often make it seem as if the motive for it has to be ethics *or* profits: executives pursue greater corporate responsibility either because they are ethical—and this will cost them in the form of lost profits—or because it makes good business sense, in which case ethics has nothing to do with it.

A growing cadre of environmentalists argues that sustainable business makes good economic sense and should be pursued where and when it is profitable. Ironically, the implication is that we should not expect executives to do the right thing if it costs the company a single penny more. McDonough and Braungart, Paul Hawken, Amory Lovins, and L.

Hunter Lovins make a compelling case for redesigning our economic system to be consistent with how nature works. The logic and examples they use show the profitability inherent in social and environmental performance. But if it is that easy, why aren't companies already adopting such green approaches? And why are some companies, such as Toyota, willing to invest in such technologies as alternative sources of energy (to the tune of 40 million kilowatt-hours of electricity in California alone) and hybrid cars (over 36,000 Priuses sold by 2002) when there is no short-term payback?

In a further ironic reversal of roles, a growing cadre of executives argues that sustainable business is simply the ethical thing to do and that it will produce enduring shareholder value in the long run. Corporate responsibility, they state, can stem only from a commitment to moral values, and seeking to make it profitable is neither convincing nor appropriate. In the June 2002 *Harvard Business Review*, Auden Schendler tells the story of Aspen Skiing Company's commitment to the environment. A proposal to retrofit lighting in a hotel garage that would cut electricity use by 65 percent was repeatedly turned down as long as it was argued in economic terms. The retrofit showed a high payback, but its champions weren't able to convince management that the project was justified. Finally, many years later, the project was approved simply on the basis of ethics. Writes Auden Schendler,

> If the economic argument didn't work, what could I do? I needed another tool. In the end, I argued that the retrofit supported our corporate values.... The bottom line: Corporate Sustainability won't occur without a company mandate that springs from ethics, not economics. Aristotle asked what it means to lead the moral life. Before business even approaches sustainability, that question will need to move from the classroom to the boardroom.[8]

The business logic of sustainability—the theme of this book—is not about choosing ethics or profits. The only sustainable business paradigm that will be both robust and compelling is one that combines shareholder value and stakeholder value. This requires a new way of seeing the world—one that will redefine the purpose of business within a democratic market system able to satisfy shareholders as well as all other stakeholders.

Creating a New Consciousness

If visionary Walter Russell were alive today, I believe that he would bring his spiritual, artistic, scientific, and managerial talents to the task of creating a planetary consciousness. The problems faced by business as an institution are not only, or even primarily, engineering or analytic problems. Many impending economic, social, and environmental crises are technically solvable. For example, it is estimated that 2 billion people live on the edge of starvation. With reduced meat consumption and a more efficient calorific conversion of the sun's energy into food, every human being on earth could easily be fed with the minimum 1,800 calories per day, using only current resources. What is missing is the mind-set and will to act.

Planetary consciousness requires a capacity to see the situation on this planet in its multiple dimensions. Managers will need to experience the world differently, as human beings connected to the world around them and not only as professional managers. As described in Part II, Patagonia's senior executive trip to the cotton fields of the San Joaquin Valley in 1992 was such a transforming experience. Without experiencing environmental degradation, or seeing firsthand the individual stories of poverty and disenfranchised communities, the shift in mind-set remains conceptual. As Yoda says in *The Empire Strikes Back,* we must "learn to unlearn" and, if we are to move the immovable, as Luke Skywalker did, then we must access previously untapped energies and believe what we have not dared to believe is possible. Chapter 5 continues this quest for transforming the mind-set and organizational culture. Now we turn to market-based measures of stakeholder value.

CHAPTER THREE

What Gets Measured Gets Managed

EXECUTIVES TODAY have good reason to feel overwhelmed by the number and variety of approaches to corporate responsibility. Each global standard—such as the Caux Principles for Business (1994), the SA8000 (1998), the UN Global Compact (1999), and the Global Reporting Initiative (2002 revised)—has its own spin on accountability, business conduct, corporate governance, community involvement, human rights, and environmental responsibility.

Scientific approaches such as those promoted by The Natural Step have contributed to a better understanding of the inherent physical limits of the earth. Increased government regulations have tightened permissible levels of air, water, and land pollution. In the United States, such regulations include the National Environmental Policy Act, the Superfund law, the Toxic Substances Control Act, the Resource Conservation and Recovery Act, and the Clean Water Act. The growth of socially responsible investing (SRI) to more than $2 trillion in 2001 has helped to define so-called sin sectors such as alcohol, tobacco, and genetic engineering. In addition, voluntary approaches to corporate responsibility have produced many different types of social and environmental initiatives. It is no wonder, then, that corporate responsibility and sustainability are sometimes seen as adding complexity and cost in an economic environment that can ill afford them.

Now a new set of measures is emerging. These measures are market-driven, and they are converging on a commonly accepted definition of what it means for a company to be responsible. Called *sustainability benchmarks*, these measures are being developed in the capital markets in collaboration with NGOs and global standards organizations. In over a dozen countries around the world, a new breed of SRI rating agency[1] is abandoning the practice of screening out sin stocks in favor of assessing companies using *best-practice benchmarks* by sector. These rating agencies use the benchmarks to give companies a sustainability score, which is then sold to fund managers looking for additional information to determine stock performance. The as-yet-underused potential of these benchmarks lies in their application as a management tool to measure and manage corporate responsibility better.

Sustainability Benchmarks as a Management Tool

Sustainability benchmarks are metrics whose legitimacy comes from stakeholders—both economic stakeholders (such as customers, employees, and suppliers) and those outside the traditional value chain (such as local communities and NGOs). The metrics typically involve dozens of performance indicators organized by stakeholder group and evaluated in three ways: by policy (intention), execution (process and structure), and results (outcome). The underlying goal is to ascertain whether the company is operating to the detriment of its stakeholders, either current stakeholders or future generations of stakeholders. The measures gain further legitimacy from their development in consultation with international NGOs such as the United Nations Environment Programme (UNEP) and asset managers such as the Swiss group Sustainability Asset Management (SAM). The metrics are based on universal principles derived from such global standards as the Caux Principles and the Global Reporting Initiative.

These new metrics are asking the following questions.

- In the eyes of each stakeholder group, does the company "walk the talk" as a corporate citizen of a more prosperous, sustainable, and equitable world?

- Is the company's social and environmental performance sustainable in policy and execution, and is it better (or worse) than that of its peers in terms of results?

For example, a company engaged in electroplating is likely to be assessed at a low level of sustainability performance simply because it is in a dirty industry. At the policy and execution levels, electroplating is environmentally damaging using current technology. At the results level, however, an electroplater with an industry-low level of environmental damages and fines will be rated well in relation to its competitors.

These questions, in turn, raise classic management issues:

- What is the company's value creation strategy?
- What organizational culture and mind-set are needed?
- What is the linkage between benchmark performance and financial results?

The sustainability benchmarks are valuable as a management tool only to the extent that they help create a strategic inflection point in the organization. Managers have to understand the underlying worldview, operating targets, and externalities (social and environmental) before they can apply the measures of sustainability effectively. In other words, business purpose needs to be grounded both in the pursuit of increasing shareholder value and in responsibility for the company's social and environmental impacts.

What is exciting for business, of course, is that these metrics finally offer the prospect of measuring and managing corporate responsibility like any other business process. Executives recognize that "what gets measured gets managed." In this context, it is useful to remember that another critical business process, customer relationship management, was once in a stage similar to that of corporate responsibility today. Before Kaplan and Norton's 1992 *Harvard Business Review* article on the balanced scorecard, customer relationships were often managed on an ad hoc basis, without linking goals and objectives to operating processes and financial results. Today, customer relationship management is quantified and tracked to almost the same extent as financial management, using sophisticated software platforms that fully integrate the process at every level of the business.

Whole-Systems Approach

Many of the SRI rating agencies use between 50 and 100 performance indicators. In one case—the Sustainability Investment Research Institute (SIRIS) in Australia—over 1,200 are used! These indicators can be usefully grouped together under 20 to 30 benchmarks expressed in terms more amenable to strategic thinking.

Any single indicator taken by itself is almost meaningless for assessing sustainability. The whole idea behind sustainability is that it requires a systems approach: you cannot be sustainable in one part of the system and unsustainable in another. For example, companies that take great care of customers and employees but continue to dump toxic wastes into the environment are missing the point.

Figure 3-1 is a schematic of the sustainability benchmarks. We examine two example indicators, one focusing on the environment and the other on employees.

In Example Indicator 1, the issue of environmental incidents, damages, sanctions and fines in relation to industry averages is illustrative of the market approach. Rather than measuring absolute levels of emis-

Figure 3-1. The Schematic of Sustainability Benchmarks

sions or waste in scientific terms (for example, NO_x emissions), the question is phrased in performance terms relative to peers and assessed in terms of dollar amounts. When used as a management tool, this indicator requires a certain amount of inquiry and exploration: What fines were paid this year? Last year? The year before last? How did this compare to our major competitors? What were the details of the incidents? Who was affected, and what was the nature of the impact? Finally, this indicator must be considered together with other pertinent indicators in the environment stakeholder group to get a picture of overall environmental performance.

Example Indicator 2 illustrates the stakeholder-centric nature of the benchmarks. Employees are legitimately concerned about management's good-faith efforts to retrain, counsel, and find other employment for people during massive layoffs. In 2001, when the European food giant Danone announced it would shut down 16 of its 36 cookie-manufacturing factories shortly after reporting stronger than expected year-end earnings, tens of thousands of protesters took to the streets in France, Austria, and Italy. The public perception at the time was that Danone was not "walking the talk" in terms of good-faith efforts for its employees. A related indicator of responsibility toward employees is that the company promotes sustainable patterns of employment by giving employees skills that have long-term market value.

Each benchmark is applied differently, depending on the company and industry. In the fast-food business, sustainable patterns of employment will look very different from those in the financial services sector. In all cases, however, appropriate measures must be developed to ensure that the company is conducting itself responsibly according to each benchmark being considered.

When taken together as a system of benchmarks defined in turn by fine-level indicators, a cohesive definition of social and environmental performance emerges.

As stated earlier, these metrics are not moralistic in the traditional sense of such "sin" products or services as alcohol, weapons, or gambling. Nor do they involve philanthropy and other charitable activities that are seen as parallel to the business or as simply another cost center. Instead, the emphasis is on how a company conducts itself in the course of its normal business operations.

Corporate responsibility and sustainability are often seen as moralistic by executives, who feel exhorted to do their part to reverse such trends as global warming, declining food safety, nuclear risks, population growth, diseases of civilization, soil erosion, water scarcity, and deforestation. Although higher ethical awareness of global problems is essential, it is time to manage the new responsibilities as one would any other key performance issue. The advent of sustainability benchmarks opens new and promising avenues for business leaders committed to corporate responsibility consistent with strong business performance.

CHAPTER FOUR

Shareholder Value
and Corporate Responsibility

T HE CONCEPT of shareholder value is not always well understood in business and is often maligned outside of business. Although the motives may vary, both business and nonbusiness readers of a book about sustainability may well ask: Is shareholder value relevant as a yardstick of business performance? Futurists, social scientists, and many otherwise well-informed observers of business are finding that the public resonates with the view that shareholder value is an obsolete metric —a leftover twentieth-century practice that became overly focused on short-term profit to the exclusion of the public good. Although the debate is not new and is partially fueled by a lack of understanding of the topic, it is vitally important in the context of calls for greater corporate responsibility.

Even within the executive ranks, a spectrum of views exists. Wall Street argues that shareholder value should be the sole objective of business and that it is a violation of fiduciary responsibility to the owners and investors to focus on any other objective.

Next are those who argue that shareholder value is essential but should be a consequence, not an objective, of good management. Here is what Unisys chairman Lawrence Weinbach says about how he looks at shareholder value: "To me, if you take care of your customers, your shareholders win. The vision of the company is to increase shareholder value . . . but I don't look at it as the single reason I'm in business. I think of it as the result of what we've been able to accomplish."[1] Weinbach's words echo those of Robert E. Wood, the CEO of Sears a half-century earlier. Wood identified customers, employees, community, and stock-holders as the four parties to any business, adding, "If the other three parties are properly taken care of, the stockholder will benefit in the long run."[2] There are a number of other well-known corporate leaders for whom the driving purpose of business is to transform society or to serve a particular unmet need. George Merck II of the pharmaceutical giant Merck & Company said, "We try to remember that medicine is for the patient. We try never to forget that medicine is for the people. It is not for the profits. The profits follow." According to Collins and Porras in their best-seller *Built to Last*, such visionary companies paradoxically outperform rivals who focus exclusively on shareholder value creation.

More distant along the spectrum is the view, sometimes held in Europe and Japan, that the business of business is to serve society and the environment, and the companies that succeed in doing this will enjoy sustained development. Profits should be adequate but need not—indeed, some Europeans would say should not—be maximized. Those who hold this view often feel that Americans are too focused on shareholder value. Many observers attribute the recent downfall of U.S. companies such as Enron and K-Mart to an unhealthy obsession with short-term shareholder results.

Yet there are excellent reasons to support shareholder value as the yardstick underlying economic, social, and environmental per-formance. It is a unifying measure that integrates economic, social, and environmental performances that would otherwise involve different benchmarks and terminologies. A company's departments of EH&S, community relations, and finance, as well as line managers, can all use shareholder value as a shared measure and as a common tool for com-municating business performance.

Shareholder value does not predispose a company to greed or irre-sponsibility. It has no intrinsic bias against stakeholder satisfaction and, unlike conventional generally accepted accounting principles (GAAP) and Financial Accounting Standards Board (FASB) accounting, its mea-surement is in theory transparent and unambiguous. The problem is not with the shareholder value concept itself but with its application: true sustainability revenues and costs are often left out of the appropriate shareholder value calculations. We will explore these problems of implementation in this chapter.

Using shareholder value as the yardstick of performance also corresponds best to the reality of global financial markets: capital gravitates to where it will earn the highest return for its owners. A company with high environmental and social standards but low shareholder value will eventually be driven out of business. This is an inescapable fact of the market system. (One could argue that the market system itself is sub-optimal, but that discussion is outside the scope of this book.)

Dennis Minano, the outgoing vice president of public policy and chief environmental officer at General Motors (GM), recently described the future of an integrated, data-driven shareholder value approach to EH&S performance in his organization.[3] GM is known for "doing the math," even on visionary new technologies fraught with uncertainties. This type of quantified approach to environmental and social issues is being adopted by a growing number of companies: British Petroleum (BP), Shell, Lafarge, Celanese, Georgia-Pacific, Hewlett-Packard, Baxter, and The Co-operative Bank, to cite a few well-known cases.

The WBCSD has built its methodology of working with leading companies using a shareholder value approach. As early as 1996, it published a report entitled "Environmental Performance and Shareholder Value" that offers a compelling framework, including value drivers—such as stakeholder satisfaction—that contribute to dividends and share price.

The growing success of INNOVEST—whose CEO, Hewson Baltzell, is a former investment banker—is further testament to the demand for financial quantification of social and environmental performance. This demand is also being met by investment rating agencies such as Total Social Impact (United States), Core Ratings (France), and SIRIS (Australia). These agencies specialize in the sustainability performance of companies in funds run by investment managers who seek additional leading indicators of shareholder value.

What Exactly Is Shareholder Value?

Shareholder value is the *net cash gain* to the owners of the capital employed in a business. The notion of net cash refers to the actual transaction of taking money out of the owner's pocket—or out of a savings account or U.S. treasury note (T-bill) where it is earning the prevailing interest rate—to buy shares of a company, and putting that money plus dividends back into the owner's pocket. As early as 1890, the economist Alfred Marshall stated, "What remains of his [the owner's] profit after deducting interest on his capital at the current rate may be called his earnings."

Shareholder value = Cash gain on capital *minus* cash cost of capital

This indicator gives the true measure of the economic earnings to the investor, whether in a company or in a particular activity or project with an identifiable earnings stream.

The financial calculation of cash gain involves a process of discounting future cash flows. Cash earned 10 years in the future receives a lower weighting than cash earned this year. The discount factor is simply the market rate of interest representing the earnings rate each year compounded by the number of years involved.

By comparison, accounting forms of profit such as net income after taxes are record-keeping conventions and do not tell the owner what he or she will actually get back on his or her investment. In the United States, these conventions follow the generally accepted accounting principles set out by the FASB.

What Happens When Different Managers Use Different Accounting Measures?

Consider how different parties often use different measures of business performance and how this practice leads to confusion when one group communicates with another group.

• Business unit managers often use GAAP forms of profit such as

sales minus costs before depreciation, taxes, and interest to judge
how well they are doing.

- Divisional managers may use another set of accounting measures
  such as net income returns on assets (ROA). This practice helps
  them not only to capture measures of profit from ongoing
  operations but also to monitor how well their division is using
  its assets.
- Executives at the board level are likely to track earnings per share
  and the company's stock price, as well as still other accounting
  conventions such as net income returns on equity (ROE) and
  net income returns on invested capital (ROIC).
- Government agencies, EH&S personnel, and NGOs may use a
  variety of nonfinancial benchmarks of social and environmental
  performance, such as indicators from the Global Reporting
  Initiative, ILO Conventions, or The Natural Step Four Systems
  Conditions.

Underlying all these interest groups is the question of value creation.
Only shareholder value accurately reflects performance for every decision or project throughout the company, from operations to compen-
sation schemes to capital investments to environmental and social
performance.

The Need for a More Relevant Application
of Shareholder Value

The difficulty with shareholder value is that its application involves
choosing revenue and cost streams, many of which are excluded from
traditional business calculations. Shareholder value calculations that
exclude such environmental impacts as pollution, waste disposal, and
loss of biodiversity are incomplete. The same is true for value calculations that fail to account for social exclusion or worsening community
relations. Companies in diverse sectors—such as Patagonia, Lafarge,
General Motors, Celanese, and The Co-operative Bank—are tracking

social and ecological performance in terms of costs to the company and monetizing the benefits through increased customer loyalty, employee motivation and turnover, and investor preference. They are also working with local and national governments to level the playing field by changing accounting practices to force their competitors to disclose the true sustainability costs of their operations.

Shareholder Value in Site Remediation: An Example

The example of Lafarge (a cement and construction materials company) is helpful in illustrating this principle. Sustainability performance for this company involves a range of issues including CO_2 emissions, human rights, employee stock ownership participation, and rehabilitation of quarries. The last issue provides a vivid illustration of how shareholder value calculations have become instrumental in measuring and managing stakeholder performance.

Lafarge operates more than 800 quarries around the world. They are located in a variety of geographic regions. The Lafarge Group views quarry rehabilitation and restoration as a priority at all sites, generally going well beyond regulatory requirements. In 2001, with the participation of the World Wildlife Fund (WWF), Lafarge adopted a formal Quarry Rehabilitation Policy to spread best practices in terms of quarrying work and relations with local stakeholders.

Lafarge, like most companies with mining activities, began rehabilitating quarries because it had to. It was a need that came from tougher legal requirements, cost avoidance, and the wish to avert negative publicity. The company found itself opposed by local communities, permitting agencies, and pressure groups that threatened a range of actions as well as negative publicity if it left its quarries in a poor state after closure.

When the logic of shareholder value was applied to quarry rehabilitation, Lafarge's senior management saw that this remediation activity is a source of value creation rather than just a constraint of doing business. This recognition then increased internal ownership for the idea of pursuing rehabilitation beyond the requirements of compliance. It also reduced the "language gap" between environmental managers and quarry line managers and helped communicate the reasons for spending more money on this activity than required by law.

The following four logics for rehabilitating quarries are unified by a common yardstick: shareholder value creation. Euro figures are given for illustrative purposes only and in some cases have been deliberately altered to respect the proprietary nature of this information.

LOGIC 1: PERMIT-RELATED ADVANTAGES

1.1 Longer-duration permits = added years of cash flow on the same initial capital expenditure and more stable market presence

An aggregates quarry in France receives a 10-year permit extension thanks to environmental excellence. It is the first ISO 14001 quarry in the country. The cost of ISO 14001 certification is estimated at €40,000. The cash gain of an additional 10 years of operation is 250,000 tons/year × €1 cash profit per ton with a Net Present Value = €1.3 million discounted over 10 years.

1.2 Permits closer to market = lower transport costs

A large aggregates quarry site owned by the company receives a permit 20 miles from Paris thanks to the company's reputation for a strong rehabilitation policy. The cost advantage of being situated close to market is estimated to be €0.08/ton/mile × 40 miles × 900,000 tons/year = €2.88 million/year

1.3 Shorter permitting process = lower permit processing costs

An aggregates quarry in the United Kingdom with a beyond-compliance rehabilitation plan helps Lafarge avoid a public inquiry that would have cost an estimated $250,000.

A U.S. aggregates quarry owned by Lafarge receives a zoning permit in 1 year compared to a competitor in the same area who applies for a similar permit but is subject to a 3-year study on free silica. The estimated cost advantage for Lafarge is €100,000.

LOGIC 2: REDUCED RISK OF HIGHER RAW MATERIALS
COSTS AND PLANT CLOSURES FROM COMMUNITY
OPPOSITION AND LOSS OF LICENSE TO OPERATE =
AVOIDANCE OF HIGHER RAW MATERIALS COSTS OR
IN WORST CASE A CEMENT PLANT CLOSURE

A French limestone quarry cedes 15 years of limestone reserves in a negotiated settlement with the NGO Charente Nature to create a nature preserve using part of the quarry land. The risk of not reaching a negotiated settlement was the closure of the limestone quarry.

A Canadian quarry owned by the company is dramatically reduced in size to preserve a rare biotope. This nevertheless allows the company to continue operating the sandstone quarry. The economic benefit is a source of limestone at \$3/ton compared to \$30/ton for the next-best source.

LOGIC 3: HIGHER LAND VALUES = HIGHER ASSET VALUATION

In the United States, farmland is purchased at \$200/acre, quarried, and then rehabilitated as residential land with a lake for \$4,400/acre at a rehabilitation cost estimated at \$500/acre, leading to a net real-estate gain of \$3,700/acre on 130 acres.

LOGIC 4: ECOEFFICIENCIES = LOWER OPERATING
COSTS AND HIGHER ASSET UTILIZATION

The coordinated progressive rehabilitation of quarries as the mineral is mined allows Lafarge to keep the size of the hole relatively small. Instead of mining the reserves until the quarry is exhausted, leaving a footprint the size of the entire quarry, coordinated progressive rehabilitation restores the landscape as it is mined—a kind of just-in-time site remediation technique. Using this method, the overburden and waste rock are moved once (instead of twice), reducing production costs by €1.35/ton.

Beyond-compliance quarry rehabilitation creates competitive differentiation and barriers to entry with significant cash-flow benefits from meeting society's expectations. Once all parties understand that the value created reflects the company's product, financial, *and* social impacts, the company can then pursue a site remediation strategy in the knowledge that doing so creates value for its owners.

The Limitations of Shareholder Value

Holding up shareholder value as a useful yardstick in measuring and managing corporate responsibility is not meant to imply that the market can take care of all our needs or that everything can be valued in monetary terms.

In Economics 101, we learn that an important class of activities called *externalities* remains outside the realm of market forces and typically requires government intervention. This problem is particularly relevant when property rights are ill-defined, as in "The Tragedy of the Commons." A *commons* is a tract of land owned and used by the community. In the now-famous example of livestock farmers sharing a nineteenth-century commons, each farmer added an animal to his herd to increase his private profit. When all the farmers added one animal to their herds, the result was collective overgrazing—a public cost. What appeared reasonable from each individual farmer's perspective quickly destroyed the commons. In such cases, only by the introduction of "government" into the picture—in the form of taxes, bans, moral suasion, standards, and so forth—can externalities be managed in a way that reflects social costs and benefits in addition to private costs and benefits.

An underlying theme of this book is that the line between private and public costs and benefits is becoming blurred. The market is internalizing activities that were previously considered externalities. Industry's emission of greenhouse gases is a good example. The rise in greenhouse gases could be considered a modern tragedy of the commons. Any one company can emit carbon dioxide (CO_2) without individually suffering negative consequences. Therefore, no company has felt compelled to take responsibility for the collective harm caused by many companies releasing greenhouse gases. The big coal and big oil lobbies of the 1990s are a testament to this denial of the emerging science of climate change. Yet the advent of CO_2 credits, CO_2 trading mechanisms, class action lawsuits, investor and consumer pressures, and the risk of damaged corporate reputations now lead many companies to reduce CO_2 emissions for reasons of shareholder value. In May 1997, John Browne, the CEO of BP, gave a landmark speech at Stanford University in which he acknowledged the potential destructiveness of global climate change. In many ways, this speech heralded a broad-based change in how big coal and big oil viewed the issues.

Many big companies remain hostile to evidence of climate change, and yet all face the risk of eroding shareholder value if they contribute to greenhouse gasses. For an example of the potential shareholder impact of CO_2 emissions, consider the case of Exxon Mobil. A study by Claros Consulting argues that this giant oil company compares badly with its peers Shell and BP for its hard-line stance on global warming. The report, by Mark Mansley, former Chase Manhattan analyst and head of Claros Consulting, claims that Exxon Mobil risks losing up to $50 billion worth of stock market value as a result of damage to its reputation and trade. Although this figure is controversial, it highlights the private value at risk from negative public impacts.

Corporate performance against a broad range of stakeholder issues—from human rights to toxic site remediation—is now being measured and turned into cash streams (either positive or negative) because society's expectations are being internalized in the marketplace. Although many people fear the monetization of our values and responsibilities, the fact that companies are increasingly including stakeholder impacts in the calculus of business is moving the global economic system in a more sustainable direction.

CHAPTER FIVE

The Stakeholder Mind-Set and Culture

THE TRANSFORMATION of mind-set and organizational culture to include key stakeholders is what enables sustainability to become an essential part of business conduct. The goal is to have sustainable development become an organizational capacity that exists at all levels from the factory floor to the executive suite. The effort to develop such a capacity must be seen as good for business, however. This in turn requires reexamining existing beliefs, rules, and behaviors that assume that caring for anything other than maximum short-term profitability is bad for business.

A deeper understanding is needed of the impact of the business on the environment, on the community, on employees' lives, and on all the other stakeholders. This understanding will come through new relationships with the key stakeholders, as well as through new insights into the meaning of "value," "brand," and "strategic capital." It will require a redefinition of the corporation that goes beyond the ownership model or the neoclassical view that firms are microscopic economic actors at the mercy of market forces. Here is one useful reformulation based on the stakeholder view:

> The corporation is an organization engaged in mobilizing resources for productive uses in order to create wealth and other benefits (and not to intentionally destroy wealth, increase risk, or cause harm) for its multiple constituents, or stakeholders.[1]

45

The stakeholder view of the firm broadens the knowledge base needed to succeed in business. It requires familiarity with entities outside of the economic value chain, from federal agencies such as the Consumer Product Safety Commission to sustainability standards organizations such as Social Accountability International. The firm must also know about voluntary cooperatives and what they are doing in response to the challenges of social disparity, environmental degradation, poverty, and the growing backlash to globalization. This broader knowledge base becomes the foundation for the firm's sustainable value creation process.

Sustainability Is a Worldview

So what is the context that allows for a business to operate sustainably?

The foundation is a worldview that recognizes the interdependence of business and its stakeholders and the systemic nature of that interdependence. It starts with the belief that we are part of a larger system—a business ecology—and extends to a willingness to examine the larger socioeconomic system and how we impact it at the individual, community, and organizational levels, and eventually at the planetary level. It challenges the prevailing belief articulated over 30 years ago by Milton Friedman, the Nobel Prize–winning economist, that "the only social responsibility of business is to make profit," as well as all the associated explicit and implicit rules that go along with that fundamental belief.

Three elements recur in the experiences of companies that have successfully transformed their corporate cultures. Taken together, these three elements open up new possibilities for the organization to work with its stakeholders to achieve extraordinary results in terms of an integrated bottom line. They represent shifts in the areas of learning, innovation, and partnership.

LEARNING

Organizational learning requires the development of a systemic capacity. Although it also requires the capacity for individual learning, as a system it involves higher-level skills and competencies. In other words, the ability of an organization to learn is more than the sum of the individual learning abilities of its employees and staff. The organizational capacity to learn requires practices and processes that open up channels of communications and learning within the system and that transform the nature of those communications from one-way information transfer to joint inquiry and dialogue. Perhaps most fundamentally, it requires a cultural shift from avoiding or hiding mistakes to embracing and learning from them. This particular shift is intrinsically opposed to the hierarchical and controlling model of organizations and requires sustained support and broad participation to be feasible.

The learning process opens up new possibilities for the organization's view of itself and its stakeholders. Stakeholders become partners in the inquiry for sustainable value and the search for innovation.

INNOVATION

Innovation requires the ability to challenge the rules, both implicit and explicit, that exist in the corporate culture. It requires an environment where change is welcomed and supported and where new ideas are given a chance to germinate and be prototyped and then implemented. The openness to new ideas extends to all the stakeholders of a process or product, from customer to supplier, and includes their ideas and feedback for creating and redesigning products and processes to reflect the values and principles of sustainability. In the stakeholder view, innovation increasingly arises in partnerships inside and outside the company.

PARTNERSHIP

The most critical paradigm shift in terms of considering stakeholders is to shift from *"us versus them"* thinking to thinking about the larger *"us."* A shift is needed from the transactional perspective to a partnership perspective. The firm must expand its thinking from "control" to "attraction" and "inspiration."

Companies that are interested in attracting the most loyal customers, the brightest employees, and the most innovative suppliers will readily see that what is most attractive to stakeholders is to be involved and engaged as true partners to the business. The relationship is based on contribution and value in both directions, which inspires further innovation and commitment and becomes a self-reinforcing spiral toward positive business results.

Customers as Stakeholders

Customers have become the most recognized stakeholders in business since Peter Drucker and Edward Deming began forcing management to see them not just as entities to be sold to but as human beings with values, ideas, loyalties, and needs. Wouldn't it serve each business to leverage that latent power and incorporate it into its processes and decisions? Answering this question has helped to fuel the "customer revolution." Interestingly, this revolution has occurred not because business all of a sudden had a humanistic concern for customers but because it was proved that customer satisfaction impacts business performance and produces positive financial results.

The global crisis of sustainability is extending that lesson to all the other stakeholders, and the sustainability benchmarks described in Chapter 4 are helping to demonstrate the positive relationship between financial performance and stakeholder satisfaction.

In addition, there is a growing recognition that there is in fact a relationship between customers' purchasing and investment behavior and their values. The growing number of cultural creatives (in Paul Ray's nomenclature[2])—as opposed to traditionalists and modernists—in North America demonstrates the power of the new "enlightened" customers and illustrates how they are influencing the forces to which corporations must respond.

A major milestone in the change of consumer values occurred after September 11, 2001. In March 2002, the *Harvard Business Review* reported on these changing values. The study was conducted by Cone, a philanthropy consulting firm in Boston that surveyed more than 1,000 U.S. consumers in March 2001 and then again in October 2001. The results show a large increase in the importance that people placed on a company's support of charitable causes. The survey asked people to complete the statement, "I place importance on a company's support of charitable causes when I . . ."

> *. . . decide what to buy or where to shop*
> Before September 11: 52 percent
> After September 11: 77 percent
> *. . . decide where to work*
> Before September 11: 48 percent
> After September 11: 76 percent
> *. . . decide which companies to invest in*
> Before September 11: 40 percent
> After September 11: 63 percent
> *. . . decide which companies I would like to see doing business in my*
>   *community*
> Before September 11: 58 percent
> After September 11: 80 percent

These results suggest that a large change in public attitude toward the social role of business—in favor of greater philanthropy—occurred after September 11. This change is part of a trend in consumer behavior toward incorporating a package of issues in how brands, products, and services are selected. In a broad range of industries, from home furnishing to financial services and food and many sectors in between, price and technical features are no longer the sole determinants of the decision to buy.

People-Centric Organizations

Fortunately and coincidentally, there is another revolution under way, albeit a quiet one, converging with the philosophy and aims of the customer revolution. This revolution is focused on the employee and represents the quest for a true people-centric organization. For some time, people have been studying, analyzing, consulting for, and improving corporations in the search for a more humane organization. The trend is away from the legacy of the Frederick Taylor paradigm (which presents a coldly rational "scientific management") and toward one in which both the organization and the human being, the individual self, flourish and prosper. That trend has required organizations to adopt nonscientific methods (much to the chagrin of industrial engineers) and to include and account for the human spirit, people's spirituality, core human values, and all the other essential forces that make us human and allow us to grow and thrive. Many studies have been done of great places to work, showing among other things that the *intangibles*—such as relationships, communication styles, leadership styles, and many other such levers—have an enormous influence on the *tangibles* measured in terms of business results. As Peter Senge says in *The Dance of Change*, "The process of strategy is not about ideas, but about releasing energy."

Values at the Core of Sustainability

Values spring from the deepest core of what it means to be human. Values hold together families, communities, and cultures, yet organizations have ignored this fact for decades. Only now are we beginning to realize that the foundation for new organizational models has to be the way corporate values are developed and implemented.

Paul Ray, Don Beck, and others are documenting profound shifts in values all around the world. In "A Revolution in Values," Neva Goodwin of Tufts University writes that basic human values have been trampled by commercial values and that "the stage is set for a moral rebellion." Better understanding the shift in values "is of critical importance for the future ability of human societies to provide meaningful life options for their citizens without destroying the ecological basis for our prosperity, or restricting human goals to the wants that coincide with the producers' need to sell their output."[3]

A survey of consumers conducted by Roper Starch Worldwide in the early 1990s classified consumers in several countries with respect to their environmental attitudes and behaviors. The survey identified five categories of consumers:[4]

1. *True-blue greens* are those consumers who have "strong personal concerns about the environment, and they are convinced that individ-

ual actions can make a difference in helping to protect and improve the environment."

2. *Greenback greens* express "commitment to the environment by [their] willingness to pay significantly higher prices for green products. But, unlike the true-blue greens, they are not likely to get involved in proenvironment activities, such as recycling, that would consume much of their time."

3. *Sprouts* show "middling levels of concern about environmental problems, but their involvement in certain kinds of environmental responsible activities can be rather high."

4. *Grousers* are those consumers who are "relatively uninvolved in proenvironmental activities, and they justify their indifference by citing factors beyond their control. By nature they tend to believe that environmental problems are caused by others and not themselves."

5. *Basic browns* make up the least environmentally active group. "While they might be concerned about pollution problems, they are convinced that their individual behavior can't make a difference in solving these problems. Thus, unlike the grousers, they do not feel the need to rationalize their lack of effort."

The Roper Starch study found that in the United States, true-blue greens grew from 11 percent to 20 percent between 1990 and 1993. On the other end of the spectrum, the basic browns grew from 28 percent to 35 percent over the same period. Like the Paul Ray study, the results suggest an increasingly sharp segmentation of consumers that represents a growing marketing challenge for many businesses.

Values have an enormous potential to tie the aspirations of all stakeholders (not only consumers) to their commitments and to create loyalty to a company and its products or services. Values elicit the emotional and philosophical component that is at the heart of human creativity and aspiration. When corporate values and individual values are aligned, breakthrough performance is a natural result, rather than something the business demands.

Values can also become the language that humanizes relationships

﹍all the stakeholders, not just customers and employees but also partners, suppliers, communities, and other formalized entities. Values serve as the common ground from which all dialogue begins, and they shape and guide the actions that are taken with stakeholders.

Business Partners as Stakeholder

Key stakeholders in the larger ecology of business are the company's various partners along its value chain (suppliers, distributors, alliances). The sustainability worldview recognizes the mutual responsibility and accountability between the company and its value-chain partners. The relationships and partnerships with businesses outside the organizational boundary are a source of creativity and innovative breakthroughs in performance, not to mention goodwill and loyalty. This perspective allows the company's partners to be engaged in critical steps of the planning and execution process. Rather than being a burden on the business, this engagement becomes a source of higher levels of performance and the creativity required to achieve that performance.

No longer are partners "vendors" to be squeezed and manipulated for the best price. Instead, they are partners in the truest sense: included at the beginning of processes, codesigning and cocreating ideas for improving business operations, and contributing to the culture of the business system. Their talent, passion, and ideas are leveraged for the profit of both partners. This type of open-boundary approach is already being practiced by companies such as GM—which, for example, includes suppliers in designing waste removal systems for their own products. This in turn influences the original design of the suppliers' products and leads to innovation for the business partner, cost savings for all, and a demonstrable commitment to sustainability.

The Community as Stakeholder

Sustainability requires an investment approach to community partnerships, whether they are local or global communities, and values the investment in terms of its future returns, both tangible and intangible.

It requires a deeper interest in and understanding of the issues and concerns of the community as a whole—that is, a systemic approach. A creative method of partnering is needed that addresses community concerns and their root causes.

A sustainable approach must teach people how to fish rather than just giving them a fish. Such an approach creates opportunities for learning and collaboration that enable a community to solve its own problems, often with the help of the intellectual power of the corporation and some seed capital. Whether a project involves constructing sewer drains in a remote village where workers live or mentoring inner-city children, the roots of the company expand into the community and help to build "relationship capital" that influences the employees' well-being and therefore their behavior.

As we increase our understanding of the larger business ecology, what emerges is a complete and reinforcing framework for stakeholder relationships. The framework can be viewed as a web of relationships, each one empowering the others in many direct and indirect ways. It is a complete framework in that each critical stakeholder is addressed and accounted for by focusing corporate attention on all the diverse stakeholders and their needs. The framework also brings to the corporation energy, creativity, and "brand-building" value from many diverse and rich sources.

Many midsize, often privately owned, companies—such as Tom's of Maine, the Body Shop, Ben & Jerry's, Patagonia, Bulmers, Green Mountain Power, Interface, Esprit International, and The Co-operative Bank—have experienced the extraordinary and lasting visibility that stakeholder engagement can bring. What remains to be seen is how the analysts on Wall Street begin to shift their worldview to encourage rather than punish such innovative practices in the larger public companies that are subject to short-term earnings pressure. It is precisely the shift in the capital markets that is the most promising sign of what a growing segment of the buying public, who are both customers and stockholders, really want. One of every eight dollars invested in North America is now placed in socially responsible funds, and these funds are growing rapidly.

The chapters that follow include case studies in industries including specialty outfitters, heavy industry, financial services, and beverages. Contrary to popular perceptions, the business value of social and environmental performance is not limited to such industries as chemical manufacturing. The journey of each company in its search for sustainable value is presented, including all the struggles and failures it encountered. As one of the UK executives of Bulmers said to me, the interest of a case study lies at least in part in telling the story "warts and all."

PART II

Companies Creating Sustainable Value

PART II

The corporate studies in this section illustrate the new logic of sustainable value, in which marketplace opportunities for stakeholder satisfaction are converging with a new ethics to make a solid and compelling case for greater corporate responsibility. The material was written with direct, open, and transparent access to the senior management of the companies involved.

The goal of the collaboration was to tell each company's story "warts and all." The stories highlight cultural transformation (Patagonia), the risk of missing strategic conditions (ARCO), sustainability branding with customers (The Co-operative Bank), and the business challenges and financial pressures faced by internal champions of sustainability (Bulmers). All four case studies vividly illustrate the idea that meeting demanding social expectations provides ample opportunities but also major obstacles for competitive advantage and increased shareholder value.

The following four corporations were studied:

Patagonia: specialty clothing and equipment
Atlantic Richfield Corporation (ARCO): oil and gas
The Co-operative Bank: financial services
Bulmers: beverages

Case studies were selected to illustrate a broad scope of application. They include one large company (with $12 billion in annual sales), two niche players, and one midsize global player. The business sectors include specialty goods, heavy industry, financial services, and consumer products.

Market pressures for sustainability require companies to integrate stakeholder strategy into the fabric of their business operations—from the products and services they sell to how they conduct themselves in sourcing, producing, and selling those products and services. Implementation can no longer be limited to philanthropic initiatives. A company that damages the environment, engages in sweatshop practices, lacks transparency, or is involved in community lawsuits will not be redeemed by its contributions to charities.

Part II tells the stories of a handful of pioneering companies that have managed, for better or worse, to integrate sustainability into the fabric of their businesses.

CHAPTER SIX

Patagonia, Inc.

WHEN MICHAEL CROOKE, president and CEO of Patagonia, Inc., presents his company to a room full of MBA students,[1] you get a visceral insight into the soul of the organization. As the room quiets and the lights dim, a sequence of breathtaking slides is projected on the large screen: the eerie mountains of the Patagonia range, wild rivers, and pristine meadows. These images are followed by shots of outdoor sportsmen: a skier telecoptering off a corniche, a kayaker taking the perfect lip in a steep fall, and mountain climbers on vertical ice-and-rock, some of whom, it turns out, are employees of Patagonia.

This love of nature and this fanatical commitment to sport are uncomplicated: they aren't about selling something or about market positioning. They are simply at the core of the company's identity. They express themselves in Patagonia's belief that the mainstream business model as we know it is unsustainable. Michael Crooke is crystal clear about this: his company follows a different drummer—and that is nature itself, the ecosystem with its closed-loop processes and celebration of diversity. Its mission statement cuts the business audience no slack: "Patagonia exists as a business to inspire and implement solutions to the environmental crisis."

The silence in the room is broken only by the occasional laugh. And this company makes money? This company is growing? It looks like a fun place to work, but can it be financially sound with all this environmental activism and bare-feet-on-the-desk culture?

The answer is that this privately held company does make a profit on its $225 million in annual sales, with 1,000 employees and headquarters in Ventura, California; Paris; and Tokyo. Founder and former CEO Yvon Chouinard is said to have demanded 10 percent pretax profit, and although the company went through a major economic crisis in the early 1990s, which included laying off 20 percent of its workforce, it has rebounded to economic health.

Sources of Value Creation

There are several reasons for Patagonia's ability to combine profitability and sustainability. Perhaps the most interesting emerging source of value creation is Patagonia's relationship with its consumers. For many companies that develop sustainability practices, the consumer is the one stakeholder group that doesn't seem to translate caring into marketplace behavior. Consumers in general provide little evidence of being willing to pay more for the products of a company with sustainability practices than for a competitor's products. Usually the technically superior product at the highest quality and lowest price wins.

According to Patagonia's own market research, about 20 percent of its customers say that they choose Patagonia equipment because of its reputation and commitment to social and environmental responsibility. In the highly competitive outdoor equipment and clothes market, such a loyal group of consumers is being translated into a distinctive source of competitive advantage.

Randy Harward, Patagonia's director of fabric development quality and environmental research and development (R&D), even sees sustainability as a possible way out of a no-win game of technical differentiation at the lowest price:[2]

> Increasingly ... we are seeing benefits [of our environmental and social responsibility] from an efficiency standpoint, from an innovation standpoint. It may even offer a way out of the game that we find ourselves in, where Patagonia is in a very saturated market where it is harder and harder to differentiate. We have existed on quality and technical innovation, but

this is harder and harder to do.... We are in that game—we are participating in creating a tweak war based on technical innovation. The question is how to get out and still be interesting. Living up to environmental and social values might just be the key here.

Of course, in Patagonia's case, being in a business where most of your customers are outdoors people certainly helps with the marketing link to the environment. The company's commitment to a self-proclaimed "dirtbag" culture works well with both sports fanatics and tree huggers. And being a specialty player fits the fringe activist mold more easily than would be the case for a mainline commodity company.

There are other value-creation reasons for Patagonia's success in the marketplace. One obvious asset is the company's strong sense of teamwork, which Michael Crooke charismatically tells us was etched into his soul during Navy SEAL training when his buds carried him after he injured his foot in a swim-and-run exercise, and which now characterizes his own leadership of the company. The fact that employees are aligned on the company's mission and find it meaningful is no small asset.

Another core competence is form-follows-function design, which appeals to the simplicity and authenticity of the sports enthusiast. Being a self-styled innovation leader has forced Patagonia's employees to rethink everything from design to sourcing and distribution, leading to benefits in both environmental performance and profitability. Jackets made from recycled plastic bottles and infant clothing made from scraps left over from its line of adult clothes are examples of this lean-and-green approach. So are its elimination of chlorine bleach from cotton fabrics and its reduced use of formaldehyde.

Its innovative products have established a reputation for being extraordinarily well-made—which has allowed them to command a price premium to match and has earned them the moniker "Patagucci" in some quarters.

In addition to major developments such as 100 percent organic cotton and recycled polyester, the company has found many other ways to reduce costs and environmental impacts, from decreasing truck emissions by increasing the use of rail transportation to reducing paper waste. Using energy from wind and solar sources and designing environmentally smart buildings and retail stores complete the picture.

Practicing Social and Environmental Responsibility in Everything It Does

These sustainability practices extend to employees, business partners, and even competitors. Employees can leave their jobs at Patagonia for up to two months to work full time for a nonprofit organization . . . provided it is somehow involved in sustainability. They earn clothing credits for carpooling and can learn nonviolent civil disobedience techniques if so inclined. Patagonia has hosted conferences for its suppliers—from zipper manufacturers to fabric processors—to focus on reducing impact on the earth. And recently, Michael Crooke has discussed organic cotton conversion with a number of outdoor companies, including Nike, The North Face, and Canada's Mountain Equipment Co-op. Mountain Equipment Co-op has converted to 100 percent organic cotton and learned the entire process from Patagonia.

Since 1985, the company has donated 10 percent of its annual profits (or 1 percent of sales, whichever is greater) to hundreds of grassroots environmental groups—more than $14 million to 900 grassroots environmental groups in total. And every 18 months, it hosts a conference for environmental activists along with dozens of its own employees to teach organizing skills as a way to boost the effectiveness of direct action groups.

Together with its operating practices, these social and environmental actions reinforce the company's commitment to building a better world.

The Transformation

Seeing the world with new eyes is at the root of Patagonia's transformation to sustainability. The company's environmental practices go back to founder Yvon Chouinard's development of innovative climbing equipment for "clean climbing." Like many companies committed to environmental responsibility, however, Patagonia originally thought of environmental performance mainly in terms of regulatory compliance, reduced waste, increased efficiencies, and the like. A major change took place in 1992.

In 1992, a farmer named Will Allen took a group of Patagonia executives to see the cotton farms in the San Joaquin Valley, home to more than a million acres of cotton. When visiting one particular field, they saw firsthand the devastation caused by growing cotton by conventional methods. Essentially, what they saw were scorched-earth practices of the worst kind imaginable.

The soil is chemically sterilized and serves simply as structural support for holding the crop stems upright. Seeds are fumigated to prevent fungi. Herbicides eradicate the weeds, and pesticides exterminate the insects. Synthetic nutrients feed the plants. Other chemicals regulate plant growth and the speed of opening of the cotton bolls. Defoliants are used to kill the plants and get rid of the leaves at the time of harvesting the bolls. The soil and the numerous ecosystems embedded in the fields are destroyed for the long term—with wide-ranging impacts on human health, birds, and all life within wind drift.

And this for "pure and natural" cotton!

The experience of seeing this devastation firsthand forever changed that group's perception of the consequences of doing business by traditional means. Further statistics only helped to confirm the need to switch to organic sources. The statistics tell a frightening story: 25 percent of the world's pesticides are used in cotton growing; 20,000 deaths annually are attributed to unintentional chemical poisoning; 8.1 tons of topsoil per acre are lost annually. Yet it was not the statistics or conceptual understanding of cotton growing practices that transformed the company. Executives understood the need to operate sustainably by experiencing what was wrong with conventional practices at a gut level involving all the senses—the heart and spirit of each individual—in a way that is authentic and deeply personal.

The switch to organic cotton sourcing came out of this experience.

It was undertaken against all odds—that is, conventional agribusiness logic provided firm evidence that organic growing could not be economically competitive. The commitment of the senior management at Patagonia was in the realm of belief in an unproved possibility. The gap between that commitment to organic cotton and the reality of its present-day economics provided a source of innovation and out-of-the-box thinking that is a role model for all companies seeking an integrated bottom line.

It would be too easy to suggest that out of this fertile period of innovation, organic cotton sourcing became a runaway success for Patagonia. In fact, the company added costs that it couldn't afford during those years, leading it perilously close to insolvency. It struggled through the mid-1990s to switch Patagonia's entire product line to organic cotton. It worked closely with farmers, suppliers, and even competitors to make organic cotton farming economically feasible at every point of the value chain. According to Crooke, the company in 2002 is once again on a solid financial footing, with a clearer competitive positioning than ever.

A lesson to draw from the Patagonia experience is that "seeing the world with new eyes" became the prime mover for the leap to a new business model of sustainability. What is interesting is that even after the 1992 tour, the company has kept alive the *experience* of seeing conventional cotton practices, both for its employees and for its suppliers. The reaction of one of Patagonia's suppliers, Rob Koeppel, a textile laminator, summed up this experience at a company meeting: "I came as a representative of business; I left a citizen of the earth."

Measuring Sustainability Performance

Has Patagonia adopted and integrated international standards for social and environmental performance into its operations? How does the company know that it is reaching environmental performance standards of excellence? The answers are not completely clear. Patagonia's environmental performance philosophy is driven by internal values and beliefs ("Every time you do something right, it turns out to be good for business too"). One is led to believe that these values and beliefs translate into measurable annual goals at the level of product development teams but that standardized performance measures based on emerging global standards are not yet an integral part of its business.

Could Patagonia's market wisdom apply to mainstream businesses, those involved in less environmentally linked products and services? Michael Crooke's reply is adamant: from his perch on top of the world, there is no reason that any company, no matter what its sector, couldn't follow this same mixed route to integrated bottom-line success.

Unlike the other examples of sustainable value creation presented in this book, Patagonia has succeeded in translating social and environmental performance into business advantage without an apparent driving focus on shareholder value. Patagonia is driven primarily by a shift in mind-set and organizational culture and by its declaration of commitment to a sustainable world. That is precisely what makes it interesting in the business case for sustainability. Yet to continue to succeed with its social and environmental positioning in the marketplace, Patagonia now needs to pay fuller attention to the strategic and financial drivers of value creation, as the next case highlights.

CHAPTER SEVEN

The Atlantic
Richfield Corporation (ARCO)

ALTHOUGH LESS WELL KNOWN than Shell or BP, ARCO (with $12 billion in annual sales) was one of the earliest major oil and gas companies to integrate social and environmental responsibility into its business strategy.[1] In 2000, ARCO was acquired by BP, which continues to lead this industry's search for sustainable value.

In the late 1960s and early 1970s, a series of events forever changed the attitudes of officers and directors of U.S. corporations, ARCO among them. The consequences of covering over Love Canal and the discharge of millions of gallons of crude oil into Santa Barbara Channel were far-reaching and permanent. Before that, there had been pockets of environmentalism, but none of the environmental groups had a following large enough to influence corporate conduct. As a result of the Santa Barbara oil spill and Love Canal, environmental legislation at both the state and federal levels followed immediately and spread throughout other developed countries. Environmental groups that supported this effort became a major force in the world.

Prior to the Santa Barbara spill and other corporate mistakes that followed, officers and directors had focused almost exclusively on the quality of their products and the profits to be extracted from the marketplace. Even the health and safety of a company's employees, contractors, and neighbors were not high on the corporate agenda; and when environmental issues were addressed, they were dealt with at the plant level, not as a major corporate policy. Sustainable value had meaning only in the context of business-for-the-sake-of-business, sustainability was not a word in the corporate lexicon, and responsible corporate conduct generally meant supporting a local charity or the CEO's alma mater.

In that era, the shareholders of Atlantic Richfield Company, a medium-size oil company, elected as their president a quite extraordinary man who had no oil industry background. Thornton Bradshaw had been a Harvard professor and a New York financial consultant before joining ARCO. This was both a blessing and a burden, since he was perceived as an outsider whose ideas ran counter to the established practices of the industry. This of course created conflicts with other oil industry leaders, but Bradshaw's unconventional approach to corporate responsibility enabled ARCO to become the sustainability leader of its industry 20 years before others fully understood the transition through which society was moving.

There were many milestones along the way that demonstrated how different Bradshaw wanted ARCO to be. With the discovery of the largest oil field in North America in Prudhoe Bay, a pipeline across Alaska was essential. Opposition created by events such as the Santa Barbara spill, however, almost doomed the project. Bradshaw realized that three radical industry changes had to occur: (1) there had to be agreement that no oil would be spilled in Alaska—and, if it were, it would have to be removed to the last drop; (2) every piece of pipe and equipment would have to be removed from Alaska after the field was depleted; and (3) environmentalists had to be invited to oversee the entire pipeline construction process.

Bradshaw believed that if a business could not withstand the very close supervision of its most severe critics, it was not likely to survive. In Bradshaw's world, financial survival and responsible corporate conduct were synonymous. Fortunately, the petroleum industry adopted Bradshaw's three proposals for change, and the Trans-Alaska Pipe System (TAPS) line was constructed.

In the early 1970s, ARCO created the industry's first corporate environment, health, and safety department. Employees assigned to this unit were technically trained to identify potential risks and to eliminate or minimize harm to the environment, to employees, and to the company's neighbors. Further, they were authorized to audit all of ARCO's operations on a three-year cycle and report their findings to the board of directors. Thus began the training of the next generation of officers and managers who would carry the Bradshaw ideals forward.

ARCO did not limit its social responsibility efforts to business-related activities. In the early 1970s, it created a foundation to direct the company's social investment efforts. At times, foundation grants approached $36 million per year, often as matching funds for amounts being donated by employees. But these grants were not traditional. A program to "adopt" public schools placed company employees in the schools, some full time, to improve the quality of education in inner cities. Another program created and funded learning centers that gave poor children choices in educational programs. Yet another project created support centers for very young, unwed mothers to provide support, health care, and educational opportunity for the mothers and their children.

ARCO was headquartered in Los Angeles, a city with a severe air pollution problem. Bradshaw organized bus routes from remote valleys and from beach communities to transport employees to and from work, thereby reducing fuel consumption and emissions. For those who could not connect with a bus, parking assistance was provided—but only if two or more employees rode in the same vehicle. The more people in the carpool, the more assistance was given. And obviously, the more people per car, the greater the reduction in CO_2 and other emissions and the greater the reduction in the need for more freeways. ARCO was also the leading supporter of rail transit in California in the 1970s. These programs and scores of others like them identified ARCO as a local, state, and national leader in innovative ideas for enhancing the quality of life while also increasing profits.

With the arrival of the 1980s, Bradshaw retired and shortly thereafter was succeeded by Lod Cook, a student of the Bradshaw philosophy of corporate responsibility. Although Cook was an industry insider, he strongly believed that the corporation had to be a community leader, wherever it did business. By the time Cook became CEO, ARCO had grown to be a global corporation and a major player in the oil industry.

One of Cook's first steps was to place an environmentalist, the retired head of The Nature Conservancy, on the ARCO board of directors. Immediately thereafter, he created an EH&S committee of the board and appointed the environmentalist as its chairman. The committee was invited and encouraged to explore any issues at ARCO that were of concern and to recommend any action that it considered necessary.

Cook came to realize that even with the steps that had been taken to establish a corporate culture of responsible conduct, ARCO was still a major participant in one of the nation's largest environmental problems: air pollution. Moreover, the city with the worst air pollution was Los Angeles, home to the largest concentration of ARCO employees and the largest ARCO refinery. Cook, like Bradshaw before him, had a range of options available to him. The industry posture was to resist change and reluctantly accept regulations and legislation that would in time compel marginal changes. Cook viewed this option as counterproductive and not in the long-term interest of ARCO, its customers, or the nation. He also recognized that population growth and the resulting increased miles driven would more than offset marginal gains from regulation.

ARCO's Venture into Reformulated Gasoline

On a particularly smoggy day in the mid-1980s, Cook was in his Los Angeles office. He reflected that he intended to remain in the city for the rest of his life and anticipated that his children and grandchildren would do the same. He is reputed to have said then that the quality of the air was not and should not be acceptable to him, his family, ARCO, or the state. He then stated that if he did not clean up the area's air, no one else could or would.

Meanwhile, during the preceding decade, federal and state regulators of air quality, as well as local agencies such as the South Coast Air Quality Management District (SCAQMD), which had authority over the Los Angeles area, had been increasingly concerned about carbon monoxide and surface ozone emissions. In the 1980s, many urban areas in California were not even close to meeting ambient standards for emission of these gases, both of which are produced by the combustion of conventional gasoline in cars. Regulators and agencies began to entertain proposals for reformulated gasoline, ethanol, methanol, electric traction batteries, and other ways of powering cars and trucks on the California roads.

ARCO launched a dedicated search for fuels that would radically reduce emissions and make Los Angeles a place where people could live without major health threats from air pollution. In August 1989, ARCO introduced its first reformulated gasoline, Emission Control One (EC-1). The formula uses an oxygenate called methyl tertiary butyl ether (MTBE) to reduce carbon monoxide and unburned hydrocarbons. In addition to meeting the oxygen requirements of the fuel, it also helps producers to compensate for the octane lost by reducing aromatics in the reformulated gasoline. Unlike ethanol, which is based on plant materials, MTBE is made from petroleum feedstocks and can be blended directly into gasoline at the refinery before distribution. ARCO immediately agreed to give the formulation for the new fuel to competitors so that they too could benefit from this significant development.

Over the next few years, Chevron, Shell, and Exxon would introduce their own versions of reformulated gasoline—but they resisted the change initially. This industry resistance meant that ARCO could not ship its clean fuels through common-carrier pipelines because the quality of the clean fuels would be compromised by ordinary fuels placed in the lines by other refiners. In a dramatic operational change, Cook decreed that all clean fuels would be delivered by truck so that the consumer would receive the best that ARCO had to offer.

Because he felt so strongly that his industry should take the major steps required to clean up the nation's air, Cook became a national advocate for clean fuels and led the effort to change state and federal laws to both authorize and require reduced-emission fuels.

In late 1990, amendments to the Clean Air Act required that gasoline sold after 1995 in nine U.S. urban areas, including Los Angeles and San Diego, would have to be reformulated to meet strict emission standards for reduced ground-level ozone. U.S. Environmental Protection Agency (EPA) regulations specified still stricter standards starting in the year 2000. In November 1991, the California Air Resources Board announced its own emission standards for reformulated and oxygenated gasoline that would go into effect in the spring of 1996. The new California standards would make the use of ethanol difficult, and as a result the majority of reformulated gasoline in California became MTBE.

Three years after the ARCO fuels were introduced in Southern California, state and federal air quality laws were changed, and Southern California enjoyed the cleanest air in recorded history. The following year was just as good.

Reformulated gasoline based on MTBE would cost more (up to 15 cents per gallon more to meet California's 1996 standards). But gasoline prices also rose significantly in 1996, leading to additional profits for ARCO and its California competitors who switched to MTBE gasoline. According to Forest Reinhardt, a Harvard professor who has studied this case, "It is impossible to verify that ARCO and its California competitors are benefiting from the regulations, since none of the companies publishes cost and profit data disaggregated by regional market, but the information that is publicly available is highly suggestive."[2]

In the year before its clean-burning fuels were introduced, ARCO sold less than 6 billion gallons of petroleum products. By 1993, product sales reached 7.38 billion gallons. In the same period, ARCO's share of the market in the five western states rose from 10.1 percent to 20 percent. ARCO became the number one gasoline marketer in the West, suggesting that corporate conduct to improve the quality of life for residents of the West had a strong beneficial effect on the bottom line.

At this point, ARCO's venture into reformulated gasoline appeared to be a clear case of win-win for shareholders and stakeholders: an environmentally cleaner product that also made the company more money and increased its market share.

Then, in 1997, a dark shadow was cast on the sustainable value potential of ARCO's clean fuel initiative. MTBE was found to have contaminated municipal drinking water in the city of Santa Monica. It was predicted that further groundwater pollution from MTBE was likely in other areas of the state. Studies—many of them questionable—were suggesting that MTBE caused cancer in laboratory animals.

None of the environmental problems was ever scientifically proved to arise as a result of burning MTBE in a car's engine. The problems lay with the handling of the fuel, and ARCO scientists fought to demonstrate that the trouble arose from leaky storage tanks rather than from the product itself when used as intended. In retrospect, it appears that science was on ARCO's side.

Nevertheless, the environmental benefits of reformulated gasoline were quickly jeopardized. An ABC radio station pounded the issue on a daily program. Ethanol producers were quick to take advantage of public skepticism, and ethanol fuel began taking market share. Widespread support for state-level legislation to ban MTBE emerged, and in August 1998 an environmental group called Communities for a Better Environment filed a lawsuit against the major oil companies.

MTBE reformulated gasoline is an example of an environmentally differentiated product that meets many, but not all, key requirements for sustainable value. Four factors made it likely that ARCO could enjoy sustained profit from this venture while creating social benefits:

1. The product itself offered both technical performance advantages and environmental advantages, potentially increasing shareholder and stakeholder value.
2. Regulators favored this particular product by the way they wrote the emission regulations for oxygenates and aromatic compounds.
3. Consumers and the environmental groups wanted cleaner-burning fuels.
4. ARCO was first to market with a product that required significant investments to modify the refinery to produce ether and to add oxygenates (ARCO spent between $300 million and $400 million in 1990 to make refinery changes).

The Achilles heel of reformulated gasoline proved to be the doubt cast on its environmental benefits. Public perceptions about MTBE's environmental risks became widespread, and to a large extent the scientific debate behind the product's environmental performance became secondary. In addition, alternatives such as hybrid gas-electric and fuel-cell vehicles are now becoming more attractive and realistic options for reducing the environmental impact of automobiles in California.

Alternatives to Gasoline

ARCO recognized that, in time, vehicles and power generation facilities would be designed to function using fuels other than those used for the past 100 years. In the 1980s, ARCO initiated a program to use biomass for fuel. This involved a serious commitment to determine whether the public or the economics would support such a venture. Unfortunately, it failed. Simultaneously, a major solar research and manufacturing process was undertaken. ARCO allocated over $200 million and some of its best minds to this project, but it too proved to be too far ahead of its time. Nevertheless, some of the technology that was developed in this venture is now being commercialized.

In the mid-1990s, ARCO determined that use of the internal combustion engine would diminish as soon as adequate alternatives were designed. ARCO, an affiliate of General Motors, and another company created a fuel-cell project to experiment with a variety of different concepts and fuel mixes. They hope to determine whether a fuel cell for a vehicle could be mass produced and whether it would offer the consumer a better alternative than the ones currently available. That project is still under way and is reaching the stage where serious testing can be undertaken. Such projects are the product of the Bradshaw-Cook concept of social responsibility.

Even while ARCO business efforts were progressing and conflicts with peers were arising, ARCO remained committed to its broad range of stakeholders. When the Los Angeles Library burned (twice), Cook raised the funds to rebuild it. When many ARCO facilities were destroyed in the 1992 Los Angeles riots, ARCO was the first to develop plans to fund minority-owned banks, create training centers, and require its employees and contractors to train minority contractors to perform required ARCO work.

By the late 1990s, it was clear to ARCO employees and to the communities where they worked that ARCO was a very special type of corporation. For the employees, there was a sense of pride that their company was different, that it did not hesitate to buck the system or the opposition of its peers, and that their employer was just as good at benefiting society as it was at making money.

In an article written for the *Los Angeles Times* shortly before ARCO was acquired by BP, Professor Xandra Kayden of UCLA wrote:

> The local economy probably doesn't need a lot of corporate headquarters to survive, but the question of leadership for the city remains. Having the resources to invest is one thing, but understanding how to help and encouraging others to follow suit is quite another. That's where ARCO excelled.

What ARCO stood for in the 1970s, 1980s, and 1990s provides a solid foundation for companies intent on creating sustainable value in the new century. No one contends that profits alone are the mark of a great business. However, unprofitable companies soon cease to be socially responsible. Social responsibility or sustainability starts with the ability to survive ethically and economically as a business, but the definition of sustainability is far-reaching and ever-changing.

ARCO was merged into BP in 2000 for strategic reasons, including the two companies' joint interests in Alaska and the worldwide consolidation of the oil and gas industry. Although corporate responsibility strategies were not a driving force in the transaction, BP's commitment to social and environmental performance helps to continue many of ARCO's earlier objectives.

In the future, profitable ventures must also improve the quality of life. Tomorrow's businesses will certainly benefit from the culture brought to ARCO by pioneers like Bradshaw and Cook, but even those pioneers of sustainability would need to modify their thinking about the role of the corporation in the twenty-first century. As the world shrinks and businesses globalize, old models will not suffice. Yet the basic values that drove ARCO will serve as the foundation for those who seek to lead in the years to come.

CHAPTER EIGHT

The Co-operative Bank

THE CO-OPERATIVE BANK, whose roots date back to 1872, is a full-service retail player in the UK commercial banking industry. Pretax profits for the year ending January 12, 2002, were $155.7 million on operating income of $660 million. The bank has 3 million customer accounts; for comparison, Barclays Bank is a major competitor with over 10 million current UK accounts. The Co-operative Bank's sole shareholder is the Co-operative Group, one of Britain's oldest mutual companies, whose services range from grocery shopping to insurance and farming.

The Co-operative Bank has produced year-on-year profit growth over the last 8 years, exceeding the UK banking industry's return on equity (21 percent in 2001, compared to 16 percent for the Major British Banking Group). During the same period, it has made ethical, social, and environmental performance a cornerstone of its market position.

According to its 2001 sustainability report, which it calls its Partnership Report, the bank's ethical and ecological positioning has made a direct contribution of around 20 percent to the company's profitability. The analysis of this value is extraordinary for its effort to link ethical, social, and environmental actions to financial results in terms of costs, revenues, and growth. It has also introduced new green accounting measures and has undertaken extensive surveys reaching 2 million customers in 2001. It has sifted through feedback from more than 60,000 respondents. The data collected and reported since 1992 on the ethical expectations of customers and the bank's performance against

75

these expectations has been linked since 2000 to increasingly sophisticated financial value analysis. For this work, the bank received the UK Social Reporting Award and the UK Environmental Reporting Award in 2000 and was the runner-up for the European Sustainability Reporting Award in 2001.

The Pandora's Box of Ethical Branding

Perhaps more than any other company cited in this book, The Co-operative Bank has made sustainability the cornerstone of its brand identity and culture. Although it speaks about social and environmental performance in terms of ethics, its approach is very similar to that of companies discussed elsewhere in this book. Therefore, in the remainder of this chapter, where the word *ethics* appears, the words *sustainability* or *corporate responsibility* could easily be substituted.

When the bank began developing this strategy in 1992, its commitment to ethics was widely viewed with skepticism. "Initially, it was alleged that ethical and environmental matters were irrelevant to the conduct of banking and financial services," says the company. By 1998, when it produced its first sustainability report, it was one of only a handful of companies to generate an independently verified account of the way value is delivered to stakeholders using principles of sustainability. By 1998, the bank was engaging in an ongoing dialogue with its stakeholders (defined below) but was finding a relatively low level of response from its employees and suppliers.

As the ethics branding strategy developed, a new challenge emerged. If you claim to be ethical in all that you do, you heighten sensitivity to conduct that may appear not to meet your lofty standards. A case in point: in 2001, only 52 percent of the bank's staff surveyed agreed that the bank behaves ethically in the way it treats them, with 26 percent stating that they felt treated unethically. Another indicator: 47 percent of staff said they "often feel under inappropriate pressure in [their] current role." What might be perceived as "just another survey result" for other companies is suddenly seen as a significant failing for a company that makes ethics its centerpiece.

The company saw the same heightened sensitivity to a range of other social and ecological performance issues, from the fact that employees with ethnic minority backgrounds make up only an unsatisfactory 2.5 percent of its workforce to increasing business executive travel during a period when its stated goal was a reduction in miles traveled per customer. Another example: in 1997, the bank had not yet begun to recycle aluminum cans. Some of the British press promptly pounced on this fact after the company issued its 1998 Partnership Report (although, generally, British press coverage of the partnership reports has been positive). What would be irrelevant in the normal course of a bank's business suddenly took on added significance because of a self-imposed ethical brand identity.

As CEO Mervyn Pedelty acknowledges, "Improving our performance year after year—across all our Partnership indicators—becomes an ever greater challenge." In recent years, the bank has had to fill in weak spots in its social and environmental performance so that its ethical positioning would appear coherent to outside observers. For example, in 1998, the company had no formal community involvement policy. By 2001, it had largely corrected this perceived weakness, although it is still working on a better measurement of the impact of its community involvement.

Because it is an office-based organization, many observers of environmental responsibility in business could well question the true value of its efforts to reduce CO_2 emissions, hydrocarbon emissions, or water use. After all, the real environmental impacts of business are found much more often in such energy-intensive industries as oil and gas or cement manufacturing. "We might be relatively small and we may not be making a huge direct environmental impact compared with some industries, but we should be leading by example," says Jayne Beer, the bank's corporate responsibility manager (or partnership manager as the bank calls it). Like Patagonia, The Co-operative Bank is committed to having an influence that is bigger than its size and to leadership by example that it hopes will eventually carry over to other sectors.

Stakeholders of the Bank

The bank's stakeholders are called partners—sustainability is about a partnership approach—and are organized into seven groups. Six of the seven are the same categories as used elsewhere in this book: shareholders, customers, employees, suppliers, local communities, and "national/international society . . . the natural world and the six billion people who inhabit it." The seventh stakeholder group is co-operators—the members of mutual societies such as the Co-operative Group, which are estimated to number over 760 million people worldwide.

Although the company is committed to serving all seven stakeholder groups, its ethical policy has quite clearly been driven first and foremost by its customers, in part "because it is generally their money that is being used, and they should have a say in how it is used." By using extensive polling and surveys, the bank has defined what is ethical largely through a deep understanding of what customers consider being ethical in business. For example, customers have helped the bank to decide to disengage from investing in certain corporate activities such as the development of genetically modified organisms (GMOs) in foods. The company declined 52 potential finance opportunities in 2001 for reasons ranging from human rights violations to animal welfare abuses and ecological damage.

In the process of conducting surveys, the bank has increased customer awareness of ethical issues and heightened customer awareness of the bank's ethical performance relative to competitors—leading, potentially at least, to a new source of competitive advantage. It has also attracted criticism in the form of perceptions that the real motives of the bank's ethical policies are simply to increase its market share. (But even if such criticism is accurate, one might well ask, "So what?")

Ethics as a Source of Differentiation

In 2001, The Co-operative Bank carried out its fourth, and most extensive, ethical policy review through a survey that reached 2 million bank customers, "possibly the largest piece of ethical consultation undertaken in the world." This research and past surveys have given the bank a detailed understanding of the role and meaning of ethical and ecological policies from a customer perspective.

For example, the company found that for 31 percent of current account customers, the fact that the bank has ethical and ecological policies is the most important reason for opening and maintaining an account. The research also suggested that ethically motivated customers are more likely to have more than one product with the bank, are more likely to recommend the bank, and are more likely to be satisfied than the bank's average customer. As part of its competitive benchmarking, the bank knows that only 1 percent of all other banks' customers open their current accounts for ethical reasons.

In 2001, the bank also published the first-ever Ethical Purchasing Index (EPI), which shows that spending on green products and services in the United Kingdom increased by 18 percent between 1999 and 2000. Produced in conjunction with the New Economics Foundation, this barometer of consumer preferences followed research published by the bank in 2000, which revealed that, in the previous 12 months, over half the population had bought a product or recommended a company because of its responsible reputation. One-third of consumers were seriously concerned with ethical issues when shopping, and one-quarter had investigated a company's social responsibility at least once.[1] The bank's research further indicates that the potential for ethical products and services in the United Kingdom could be as much as 30 percent of consumer markets. For this potential to be realized, however, there needs to be an explosion in robust ethical and environmental reporting in the United Kingdom. Trust must be earned.

The bank clearly sees the shift in consumer values and preferences as having a huge potential for differentiation. As evidence, the company points to a massive 60 percent of consumers surveyed who say that they do not have enough information about companies' social or environmental behavior to make a purchasing decision. The bank would like to correct this problem not only by providing full disclosure about its own performance record but also by influencing the reporting requirements for the industry as a whole. Full-cost green accounting and fuller disclosure by all competitors would provide it with an obvious source of differentiation.

Ethics as a source of competitive advantage comes only partially from the bank's product and service offering. How the bank conducts its business is equally important. One example among many: gender diversity is high, with 63 percent of the bank's staff being women, compared with 45 percent of the general workforce in the United Kingdom. As noted above, however, the number of staff members who consider themselves to be from an ethnic minority has remained at an unsatisfactory 2.5 percent in recent years.

How Ethics Creates Shareholder Value at The Co-operative Bank

Like Patagonia, The Co-operative Bank has made social and environmental performance a centerpiece of its brand identity and customer differentiation. This makes it possible for shareholder value to be created through increased revenues and growth rather than only through cost savings (which is typical for companies focused exclusively on process cost reductions such as decreased waste and lower energy consumption).

Process cost savings are easy to identify, but they are not the largest potential source of shareholder value creation. In the bank's case, a good example of process cost savings is in paper purchased per customer account, which fell by 52 percent (903 tons) over 5 years, leading to a savings of $5 million per year. Other savings include

- Waste per customer account has fallen by 36 percent since 1998, resulting in savings of $12,000.
- Water usage has fallen by 28 percent per customer account since 1999, leading to savings of $30,000.
- Transport-related CO_2 emissions have fallen by 6 percent per customer account after the company switched to special low-emission diesel vehicles. Savings amount to about $1000 per fleet vehicle.

THE CO-OPERATIVE BANK'S ETHICAL POLICY

Human Rights

Through our investments, we seek to support the principles of the Universal Declaration of Human Rights. In line with this, we will not invest in

- Any government or business which fails to uphold basic human rights within its sphere of influence
- Any business whose links to an oppressive regime are a continuing cause for concern

The Arms Trade

We will not invest in any business involved in

- The manufacture or transfer of armaments to oppressive regimes
- The manufacture of torture equipment or other equipment that is used in the violation of human rights

Corporate Responsibility and Global Trade

We advocate support for the Fundamental International Labor Organization Conventions. In line with these, we will seek to support businesses that take a responsible position with regard to

- Fair trade
- Labor rights in their own operations and through their supply chains in developing countries

We will not support

- Irresponsible marketing practices in developing countries
- Tobacco product manufacture
- Currency speculation

THE CO-OPERATIVE BANK'S ETHICAL POLICY, *continued ...*

Genetics Modification

We will not invest in businesses involved in the development of genetically modified organisms (GMOs), where, in particular, the following issues are evident:

- Uncontrolled release of GMOs into the environment
- Any negative impacts on developing countries; in particular, the imposition of "Terminator" technologies
- Patenting; in particular, of indigenous knowledge
- Cloning; in particular, of animals for nonmedical purposes

Social Enterprise

We will seek to support charities and the broad range of organizations involved in the Social Enterprise sector, including

- Co-operations
- Credit unions
- Community finance initiatives

Ecological Impact

In line with the principles of our Ecological Mission Statement, we will not invest in any business whose core activity contributes to

- Global climate change, through the extraction or production of fossil fuels
- The manufacture of chemicals that are persistent in the environment and are linked to long-term health concerns
- The unsustainable harvest of natural resources, including timber and fish

Furthermore, we will seek to support businesses involved in

- Recycling and sustainable waste management
- Renewable energy and energy efficiency

THE CO-OPERATIVE BANK'S ETHICAL POLICY, *continued* ...

- Sustainable natural products and services, including timber and organic produce
- The pursuit of ecological sustainability

Animal Welfare

We will not invest in any business involved in

- Animal testing of cosmetic or household products or ingredients
- Intensive farming methods, for example caged egg production
- Blood sports, which involve the use of animals or birds to catch, fight, or kill each other
- The fur trade

Furthermore, we will seek to support businesses involved in

- The development of alternatives to animal experimentation
- The farming methods which promote animal welfare, for example, free-range farming

Consumer Consultation

- We will regularly reappraise customers' views on these and other issues and develop our Ethical Policy accordingly.
- From time to time, we will seek to represent our customers' views on the issues contained within our Ethical Policy and other ethical issues, through, for example, our campaigning activities.
- On occasion, we will make decisions on specific business, involving ethical issues not included in our Ethical Policy.

On the product side, the bank offers a number of personal Visa cards supporting Greenpeace, Amnesty International UK, Oxfam, Tearfund, and Save the Children, as well as several other cards supporting cause-related marketing. Increasingly, the credit cards are offered using a special environmentally sound plastic called PETG instead of the conventional PVC.

Other ethical products and services include a green mortgage that requires the bank to make a payment to Climate Care each year through-out the lifetime of the mortgage, deposit accounts that use FTSE4Good[2] criteria to screen portfolio holdings, and business loans granted on the basis of ethical screens of the loan applicants.

In 2000 and 2001, the bank conducted extensive analyses suggest-ing that by placing ethics at the center of its brand identity, it increased its top-line revenues and growth. By attempting to capture the total profitability contribution made by its sustainability initiatives, the bank is able to include such revenue impacts as higher product pricing; a more profitable mix of customers; new personal and business accounts; higher customer loyalty leading to lower customer turnover; revenues from new products; and penetration into new business markets such as low-income areas, where it is almost twice as successful as other banks.

The company admits that it is not possible to identify the impact of ethics on its overall profitability exactly. Its initial methodology in 2000 related brand value to profit contribution and then used survey ques-tions to identify what percentage of the brand value is attributable to ethics.

In 2001, to increase the degree of precision, the bank used the prof-itability of each product as the basis for its calculation. To illustrate the 2001 methodology, imagine that a particular current account has a profit of $100 per account and there are 10 customers for that type of account. If the bank's survey results indicate that half of these 10 cus-tomers opened and maintained their accounts for ethical or ecological reasons, then $500 of the profit is attributed to the bank's ethics poli-cies and position in the marketplace.

The survey uses computers to sort the options presented to pollsters randomly to ensure that no bias arises from the order of presentation. From this survey, the bank determines that 53 percent of personal cur-rent account customers state that "ethics" is one of a number of impor-tant factors, and 31 percent cite "ethics" as the most important factor.

The profitability of each product is then multiplied by the ethical motivational factor and aggregated to produce an ethical profitability

SAMPLE SURVEY QUESTIONS USED IN 2001
FOR PERSONAL CURRENT ACCOUNT HOLDERS

Which of these factors are important in your decision to open and maintain a Co-operative Bank account? *Any number of influencing factors can be specified:*

> Branch near home/work
> Parents banked there
> Recommended to me
> Dissatisfied with previous bank
> Image/reputation
> Ethical/ecological reasons
> Lower charges/competitive rate
> Other

Which of these factors is *most* important in your decision to open and maintain a Co-operative Bank account? *Only one influencing factor can be specified:*

> Branch near home/work
> Parents banked there
> Recommended to me
> Dissatisfied with previous bank
> Image/reputation
> Ethical/ecological reasons
> Lower charges/competitive rate
> Other

contribution range (which includes those customers for whom "ethics" is the most important determining factor and those customers for whom "ethics" is one of a number of factors).[3] Because two survey questions are used—one asking for all influence factors and the other asking for only the most important one—a profit range can be calculated. The low number of 14 percent reflects only those customers who said ethics/

ecology was the most important factor in their buying decision, whereas the high number of 26 percent reflects customers who identified ethics/ecology as an important factor.

Here is a summary of the survey analysis results:

- 26 percent of the bank's profits are assigned to customers who cite ethics as an important factor
- 14 percent of profits are assigned to only those customers who cite ethics as the *most* important factor
- An average of 20 percent is then calculated

What does the bank think of these results?

The principal factor behind the improved "ethical" profitability contribution is the discovery that there is a higher proportion of ethically-motivated Corporate and Business Banking customers than previously identified. For example, new research shows that the Bank's ethical and ecological positioning is the number one reason cited by Business Direct Customers for opening and maintaining an account. Of the profitability assigned to customers who cite ethics as the most important factor, 69 percent is attributable to Personal Banking customers and 31 percent to Corporate and Business Banking customers. Of the profitability assigned to customers who cite ethics as an important factor, 61 percent is attributable to Personal Banking customers and 39 percent to Corporate and Business Banking customers.

One theme of this book is that shareholder value creation is a more relevant measure of stakeholder performance than accounting profit. As Chapter 11 argues (in Discipline 5), shareholder value uses discounted cash flows (already more accurate than accounting profit) *plus* strategic value in the form of real options (useful for capturing the uncertainty in sustainability trends) *plus* market irrationality. Although The Co-operative Bank continues to use accounting profit, it should be credited with two important innovations in linking stakeholder performance to financial results:

1. It has moved from project cost-benefit analyses, such as the additional cost of purchasing renewable energies as opposed to

purchasing fossil fuels, to a company-wide profit impact analysis. By doing so, it has helped to capture revenue and growth impacts from brand value and customer differentiation that individual sustainability initiatives typically fail to capture.

2. Its accounting systems use a fully costed activity-based management system for its product profitability and new green accounting measures.

The Co-operative Bank falls short of identifying the true shareholder benefits of its sustainability strategy, mostly for reasons related to its measurement methodology. But it does a fine job of determining the company-wide financial impact of that strategy.

CHAPTER NINE

Bulmers Limited

A successful, sustainable business plan for the long-term, looking beyond imme-diate profit, to returns that can be achieved over many years, in ways which maintain its social and environmental capital. . . . We believe there is an over-whelming business case for our engagement with sustainability, not least because our stakeholders — suppliers, customers, consumers, shareholders and all those affected by our operations — will increasingly expect it of us. There is a long way to go. But the journey has begun. (BULMERS ANNUAL REPORT, 2001)

Bulmers is the world's leading cider company, with $750 million in annual sales. It is a major player in what is somewhat awkwardly called the "long alcoholic drinks" sector, which includes hard cider, spritzers, flavored schnapps, and bubbly alternatives to beer and wine. In the United States, it sells under the names Strongbow, Woodpecker, Cider Jack, and Woodchuck and can be found in supermarket stores and Irish bars across the country. In Europe, Strongbow is its premium brand, and it also markets Scrumpy Jack in the United Kingdom and Amstel and San Miguel beers. It is a key player throughout continental Europe as well as in Australia and New Zealand.

The Bulmers family—no longer in senior executive roles—collec-tively owns over half the company's shares and has a long tradition of community leadership in Herefordshire. Two executives—Rob Garner, group human resources director, and Charlie Bower, head of sustain-ability—are the sustainability champions inside the organization, along with sustainability manager Richard Heathcote and a number of staff worldwide.

At first glance, a company in this sector has at least three things going against making sustainability the core of its business strategy: (1) the alcoholic drinks sector is a morally sensitive one not particularly known for its social conscience; (2) its consumers appear unlikely to have save-the-world purchasing preferences; and (3) the market segments in which Bulmers competes are highly competitive, with relatively low margins. These are hardly ideal circumstances for making the long-term investments that sustainability typically requires.

And yet taking on sustainability as an integrated part of its strategy, culture, and operations is precisely what Bulmers wants to do. There are no timid social or environmental gestures for this company, only occasional doubts and fears about making a business go of it. In many ways, talking to senior executives of Bulmers in the United Kingdom is vaguely reminiscent of conversations with Patagonia's managers across the Atlantic. In a conversation about the need to use metrics from the capital markets to measure sustainability performance and to ground the conversation in analytic methods, one Bulmers executive warned me about the risks of not being radical enough: sustainability, he said, needs to start with a transformation of the heart and spirit—a commitment to being sustainable—rather than a "bolt-on" analysis of social and environmental performance.

Nevertheless, in a highly competitive market, Bulmers has been forced to look closely at everything in terms of profitability—and sustainability has had to fit into this mind-set. By one insider's estimate, business survival accounts for 85 percent of the company's focus.

Launching Sustainability

In 2001, the company arranged a three-day workshop with leading sustainability experts from all over the world. Facilitated by Amory Lovins of the Rocky Mountain Institute, this meeting launched a series of initiatives aimed at making the company more sustainable. During this

A VOICE FROM THE BULMERS EXECUTIVE SUITE

I see our approach to sustainability as a twenty-first century version of the values this company has always espoused: responsibility to our society, our employees, and our wider world. I also see it as good business. I am reminded of the "principle of obliquity" which a friend of mine explained to me. Put simply, this principle suggests that some objectives are best pursued indirectly. Pursuing profit for its own sake and "making the numbers" can be hard work. However when people are pursuing something that is meaningful to them and fits with their personal sense of purpose, they release extra commitment and energy which *by obliquity* improves the company's financial performance. Philosophically and commercially, this for me is the real win-win.

Rob Garner, Group Human Resources Director

period, Rob Garner and Charlie Bower obtained what in retrospect would be called a "benign endorsement" from the executive group. In practice, this meant that sustainability as a business strategy would receive general positive support, but there were insufficient hard conversations about the investments required and the competencies needed to succeed. It was simply regarded as prudent not to create too large a disturbance when many small sustainability steps could be taken.

As a result, in 2002 Bulmers found itself challenged to make the transition from a cost-cutting and risk-management approach to a full-blown sustainability strategy involving every aspect of the business. This challenge illustrates well the phase change with which many companies are confronted during sustainable value creation—from the lower levels of strategic focus to the higher levels shown in Figure 9-1. This framework is developed further in Part III, and here we only note two key features. First, the higher levels of strategic focus are associated with potentially much higher levels of value creation than the lower levels. Second, the higher levels tend to include the lower levels—for example, organic cider (level 3) includes the redesign of environmentally responsible manufacturing processes (level 2) and risk/reputation management (level 1).

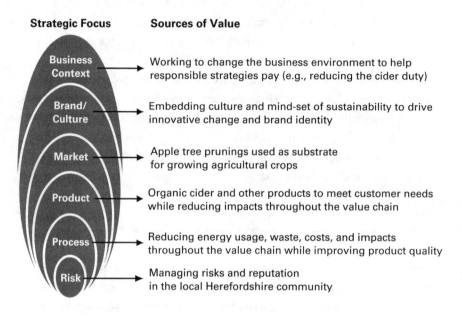

Strategic Focus

Business Context

Brand/Culture

Market

Product

Process

Risk

Sources of Value

Working to change the business environment to help responsible strategies pay (e.g., reducing the cider duty)

Embedding culture and mind-set of sustainability to drive innovative change and brand identity

Apple tree prunings used as substrate for growing agricultural crops

Organic cider and other products to meet customer needs while reducing impacts throughout the value chain

Reducing energy usage, waste, costs, and impacts throughout the value chain while improving product quality

Managing risks and reputation in the local Herefordshire community

Figure 9-1. The Bulmer's Path to Sustainability

To develop this analysis further, we look at how Bulmers achieved initial success in 2001 (Phase One) and contrast it to possible sustainability strategies it is considering from 2002 onward (Phase Two). Phase Two captures Bulmers's attempted leap to sustainable value involving its markets, its brand and culture, and its business context—using social and environmental performance as a source of shareholder value creation and competitive advantage.

Sustainability Phase One

Like many companies embarking on sustainability as a core business strategy, Bulmers started by looking for cost savings aimed at showing that sustainability could pay its own way. The idea was to generate tangible cost savings before undertaking more ambitious plans to invest in such things as brand differentiation and new sources of revenue generation. With this approach, Bulmers was able to achieve cost savings of $450,000 in 2001 and 2002 from three primary sources: manufacturing, transport, and supplier/community initiatives such as sustainable orcharding.

Sustainability Phase One Targets for Bulmers UK

- *Transport:* 75 percent reduction in environmental impact by 2004
- *Waste:* Zero waste emissions by 2003
- *Energy:* All electricity from renewables by 2002; all energy from renewables and a 50 percent reduction in primary energy consumption per hectoliter of product by 2004
- *Orcharding:* Become the leading sustainable producer of beverage raw materials in Europe
- *Human Resources:* Develop leading remunerations, pensions, and car policies for sustainability by end 2003/2004
- *Community:* Catalyze Herefordshire's emergence as a model vital sustainable rural-based community; by 2002, 20 percent of workforce involved in Foundation community projects

---

Manufacturing Cost Savings

Cost savings in manufacturing involved eliminating inefficiencies created by old approaches to product or process design, initially focused on minimizing resources used and reducing wastes.

Amory Lovins and his colleagues reportedly identified potential savings of $100,000 in refrigeration costs and $100,000 in other electrical costs. One particular pipe in the fermentation plant caught Amory's eye. It snaked across a large section of the factory with 16 visible right-angle elbows. "That pipe had 11 elbows that could be eliminated by just rotating the tank about 60 degrees around its vertical axis before hooking it up."

Overall, Bulmers cut its process energy consumption per hectoliter of product by 4 percent.

Other process-related projects include

- Diverting waste from its packaging lines from landfills. Some 95 percent of its steel, aluminum, glass, PET. and polythene is now recycled.
- Recycling postconsumer waste.
- Pomace, the pulp from the apple presses, is another bulky waste stream—18,000 tons are produced each year in the United Kingdom alone. Most of it is dried in an energy-intensive process for pectin extraction. Bulmers is now looking at composting instead of drying.
- Hundreds of millions of liters of water—along with 5 million liters of cider and smaller amounts of solids, apple juice, cleaning agents, and other materials—are discharged to sewers each year. The company has started a major drive to cut these wastes. One alternative involves lagooning followed by reed bed treatment.
- Extracting value from the 1,500 tons of apple tree prunings in Bulmers's own orchards. Environmental consultant Gunter Pauli suggested that the prunings be chipped and used as a substrate for growing agricultural crops. The value of this produce could be up to $10 million per year—more than the value of the apples themselves. Bulmers is now looking at this project more closely and is considering the possible use of the prunings as a substrate for high-value shiitake or oyster mushrooms.

TRANSPORT

The company's second biggest source of carbon dioxide and other air pollutants is transport. Since 1991, the half-million tons of finished goods that are shipped from the main Herefordshire facility every year go by road.

New trials with rail delivery have started. Richard Heathcote, the company's sustainability manager, believes that the switch would be cost-neutral while providing clear environmental benefits, particularly in CO_2 emission reductions per ton-mile of about 80 percent. Other more radical transportation solutions are under study.

SUPPLIER AND COMMUNITY INITIATIVES

Bulmers currently draws the vast bulk of its apple supplies from intensively managed orchards, with a herbicide-cleaned strip beneath the trees and four or five fungicide applications each year.

The sustainable orcharding alternative focuses on securing a better apple—one with higher quality, higher profitability, and a cleaner fruit. Experiments include using an understory of broad-leaved plants in place of herbicides; new harvesting machinery; and a revised contracting process that rewards growers for meeting key quality parameters rather than just weight of produce. Promotion of more sustainable orcharding has resulted in both community benefits and economic advantage—for example, providing greater long-term security of income to the county's farmers through local procurement of higher-quality raw materials at a lower cost to the company.

Bulmers has a long tradition of partnership within the local community of Herefordshire. Employees are encouraged to become actively involved in the local community through volunteering. Bulmers has agreed to donate $100,000 each year and 50 person-days each month to community projects to which employees are committed. The funding and time are managed by members of the employee council.

A reader may well ask how such philanthropic activities add business value. Yet in total, the company's social and environmental actions are seen, at least by some, as having contributed to a 2 percent reduction in the government's duty on cider in 2001. This duty reduction—valued at $1.6 million per year by the company—is felt to reflect the chancellor's support for Bulmers's approach to sustainability and the cider industry's links with agriculture—it accounts for over half the apples grown in the United Kingdom. Bulmers is ensuring that this money is put to use in the way intended by the government.

Bulmers was recognized in 2001 as one of "The Sunday Times Top 50 Best Companies to Work For."

BOARD PAPER NO. 1228: SUSTAINABILITY

By Rob Garner
Group Human Resources Director
30 May 2002

Introduction

This paper scopes out the steps we have taken so far on our sustainability agenda, the costs and benefits of this work; the program for this year, and the proposed agenda thereafter.

Objectives

Our Vision declares that we will become a benchmark for sustainable business. In order to do so, it is clear that we must demonstrate that our approach towards sustainability is good business. We aim to demonstrate this by

- The savings achieved by reducing or eliminating waste (e.g., water, energy, CO_2, etc.)
- The additional revenue or margin enhancement generated from products marketed from a sustainability vantage point (e.g., organic cider or cause-related marketing such as we have recently trialed in South Wales)
- The additional revenue from new types of product or business activities (e.g., mushrooms)
- The intangible benefits of improved shareholder relationships, or the attraction of new investors who are motivated by our approach to corporate social responsibility
- The risk reductions involved in developing links with government and a reputation for corporate social responsibility, which may help offset the possibility of punitive taxation or anti-alcohol legislation

BOARD PAPER NO. 1228: SUSTAINABILITY, *continued* ...

Benefits to Date

Even by the most stringent measures, we estimate that the savings in energy, steam, waste, carbon dioxide emissions, and effluent charges will have generated a return greater than our total investment in sustainability at the end of this year. If we liken this to a business start-up, our ability to more-than-fund our investment in the early years might be regarded as good business!

In addition, we have reasonable cause to believe that our work on sustainability was a key catalyst to the cider duty reduction, which produced a $1.6 million benefit.

The Agenda for Fiscal Year 2003

In order to demonstrate further the commercial benefits that can be derived from this agenda we have focused down to a limited number of specific projects:

MUSHROOMS

Complete the existing trials, which appear to be demonstrating that mushrooms can be grown in reasonable quantities on apple tree pruning substrate. Evaluate the commercial opportunity this represents; develop business plan; implement (in partnership).

ORGANIC CIDER IN UNITED STATES

Evaluate the feasibility of a brand whose provenance emanates from one or more of the following attributes:

- Vermont-ness
- Organic
- Helping the failing apple growing industry
- From a truly ecologically and socially responsible business

If appropriate, launch and test market.

BOARD PAPER NO. 1228: SUSTAINABILITY, *continued* ...

WASTE

We aim to reduce waste to landfill from manufacturing during this year to zero. This will achieve a net saving of $25,000 p.a.

We are working toward using treated borehole water for product. This will save approximately/up to $100,000 p.a. and should be partially grant funded.

ENERGY

By focusing on energy and emissions savings, as a minimum we will seek to avoid the statutory Climate Change Levy of $170,000 p.a.

In order to reduce CO_2 emissions further we are seeking more profitable alternatives to drying pomace.

TRANSPORT

We are actively pursuing use of rail for inbound glucose supply logistics. This will attract grant assistance which can be used for already planned infrastructure improvements avoiding need for capital.

TRIPLE BOTTOM LINE ACCOUNTING–

We have been working with Forum for the Future to identify the hidden (externalized) social and environmental costs toward which we may directly or indirectly contribute. The Forum has indicated that our work in this area is "ground breaking" which is giving us access to government and developing our reputation as a thought leader in this area. We intend to further our work this year with a view to being able to publish these accounts—or a digest of them—should we choose to do so.

In partnership with the Bulmers Foundation we will continue to develop our approach on a number of broader issues, including

- The development of Holme Lacy College as a leading European center for sustainable agriculture
- Working with Forum for the Future and other bodies to establish a new land use model
- Partnering other institutions to bid for a $20 million grant-aided organic processing facility in Herefordshire

• In liaison with the Herefordshire Partnership, stimulate the regeneration of Hereford City and the sustainable development of the County.

Future Agenda

Clearly our future approach will be predicated on the success of this year's agenda. We acknowledge the need to keep our efforts focused and grounded on the requirement to demonstrate commercial payback. Some of the projects we are undertaking are breaking new ground. Thus the gestation period can be prolonged and the payback uncertain.

Nonetheless we do feel that the work to-date, carried out by many people across the company, is evidencing that our sustainable development strategy is adding value to the bottom line—as well as paving the way for a much more strategic benefit in the long term as we influence government, community key stakeholders, and, most importantly, existing and new consumers.

Sustainability Phase Two

Although promising, the cost savings in Phase One were insufficient to make believers of a number of senior executives inside the company as well as of City analysts who were closely watching bottom-line performance during a slowdown in the long alcoholic drinks market. To complicate matters, against stock market expectations of a profit goal of $32.5 million for fiscal year 2002, the company was obliged to issue a profit warning during Christmas 2001 and then a further warning in February 2002, which took earnings expectations down into the $22 million to $24 million range, before ultimately posting a profit before tax of $21.1 million.

In September 2002, under intense pressure to improve financial performance, the board let go CEO Mike Hughes. Colin Brown, a former nonexecutive member of the board, was appointed interim CEO while the search for a permanent replacement was under way. Then, in December 2002, the company announced that it would cut 200 jobs and report a $1.8 million loss for fiscal year 2003. As of January 1, 2003, Miles Templeman took over as the new CEO.

During such difficult times, anything that is not perceived as directly contributing to the bottom line is naturally viewed unfavorably. Senior executives are under pressure to keep their jobs. Pro- and anti-sustainability camps develop within the executive group. Unit operating managers under pressure to deliver financial results have little attention for what they might perceive as "fluff" or at best a discretionary activity that distracts from their core objectives.

In Phase Two, sustainability champions Rob Garner and Charlie Bower are increasingly focusing their attention on top-line growth opportunities: brand differentiation, new products outside the core business, new businesses, and new financial strategies.

The Consumer Paradox: Marketing Social Responsibility to People Who Drink to Forget

It has taken some time to engage the marketing department of a company whose main product is designed to help people forget their worldly cares or simply to have fun. Some marketing managers inside the company claim that customers are just not interested in social and environmental issues. The stakes are high: marketing expenditures and the potential impact on sales are much higher than the potential gains from energy efficiencies and waste reductions.

The difficulty here is that sustainability involves an entirely new view of consumer needs and of the key success factors in brand positioning. Asking traditional marketing questions simply may not get at the potential of selling to emerging consumer segments such as those identified by Paul Ray (see Chapter 5).

The answer to the consumer paradox will look very different depending on which set of values predominates in the markets to which Bulmers is selling. If significant segments of the U.S. and UK markets are moving from traditionalist to cultural creative values and preferences (as Paul Ray believes to be the case), then combining cider's traditional marketing features with social and environmental responsibility may no longer be as paradoxical as initially thought.

Another challenge comes from the fact that the company's cider products are sold under various brands (Woodchuck, Strongbow, Scrumpy Jack, and so forth). So branding Bulmers as a sustainability enterprise would have little meaning for consumers.

The real challenge is to shift the core cider brands. . . . Conventional research says our consumers aren't interested in sustainability. I think that says a lot about conventional research. But the real issue is how to communicate a sustainability message to people who may be drinking just to forget it. That is a powerful paradox that we have to resolve. But we're determined to prove the business case of social responsibility, and you're talking about changing some fundamental assumptions and straightening a lot of intellectual pipework.

Charlie Bower

Organic apples may also prove to be a valuable marketing angle. In traditional cider making, apples are sprayed 35 to 40 times per year. Conventional marketing wisdom says that people would probably care if they knew—but that for the most part they don't want to know. The company has already launched its first organic product, Bulmers Organic, in the United Kingdom and is now exploring a product launch in the United States.

Charlie Bower is also looking at new products and new market opportunities outside of cider. The key challenge for new products is to ensure that the company has the competencies and the commercial teams needed to sell them.

An even trickier issue: alcohol abuse. "The question for Bulmers," says Charlie Bower, "is how to define our share of responsibility . . . then understand with our stakeholders how to address it." He has in mind schemes to channel a proportion of profits into social initiatives that help solve the problems the company's products help perpetuate—for example, to support abuse rehabilitation programs.

The Capital Markets: Developing Investor Loyalty Based on Sustainability Performance

Traditionally, ethical funds walk away from companies engaged in selling alcohol. However, a new opportunity may be opening up for Bulmers with the shift of capital markets away from exclusionary screens toward positive ratings based on how businesses conduct themselves with key stakeholders.

The question Bulmers is now asking is: Could the company secure a core group of investors with an emotional link to the company's values and corporate responsibility program? Securing such an investor group is seen as essential to supporting some of the long-term investments required for sustainability.

Bulmers is also intent on monetizing perceived negative externalities across a range of social and environmental issues that would allow investors to compare Bulmers stock with other stocks on a full-cost accounting basis—presumably to Bulmers's advantage once comparative externalities are known and quantified. Identifying and monetizing externalities also offers Bulmers a framework for future taxation.

Here is an excerpt from the draft Bulmers 2002 sustainability report:

We are implementing an innovative sustainability accounting framework to help us track the costs and benefits of our "internal" (i.e. expenditure actually incurred and captured within our accounting systems) sustainability investments. . . . The sustainability accounting framework is also helping us to quantify external environmental and social risks to the business and to identify avoidance and management options available to the company. Having adequate systems of internal control to enable us to do this is a listing requirement under the New Combined Code. Proposals under the Company Law Review are also likely to make the disclosure of factors affecting future business performance—including environmental and community impacts—a statutory requirement. The full sustainability accounting framework involves the production of four sets of accounts—environmental and social financial statements covering our internal performance as defined above and external social and environmental cost accounts. We hope to report the results of this developmental work more completely over the coming years.

The challenge for Bulmers involves not only the methodology for monetizing the social and environmental externalities but also the question of how to go about identifying the target group of investors. Senior management holds a genuine belief that these ethical investors do exist.

Bulmers has commissioned Forum for the Future, a green think tank, to prepare a set of environmental accounts—using a methodology originally invented for Interface, the Atlanta-based carpet manufacturer.

Making the Business Case for the Next Phase

To develop the internal support necessary for Bulmers to move forward with the Phase Two objectives, the company intends to adopt financial approaches that will help make the business case for sustainability. There is evident tension between choosing a transformative path to sustainability, which involves "seeing the world with new eyes," as Patagonia did (see Chapter 6), and choosing an analytic framework that focuses attention on the numbers at the risk of missing the larger purposes of sustainability.

The draft Bulmers 2002 sustainability report concludes:

Our challenge, however, will be to continue to demonstrate that triple bottom line ideas of corporate responsibility can gain a foothold in the face of short term market pressures. We are confident that they can. Ultimately all economic value flows from goods and services provided by the environment (natural capital) and people (human capital) themselves. These resources should not be eroded if we want to maintain and increase our ability to generate future wealth. Our aim is to operate within these limits, to reinvest in both natural and social capital and to transform Bulmers into a genuinely sustainable enterprise.

For a company whose commitment to sustainability has been described by a UK publication (the *ENDS Report,* January 2002, issue no. 324) as "probably the most searching examination against sustainability principles ever embarked on by a major British company," the only question is whether short-term stock-market hurdles will overwhelm its best efforts or the new strategy will produce tangible benefits in time.

The Value Creation Tool Kit

PART III

How can business unit heads, chief financial officers (CFOs), board members, EH&S managers, and other business professionals help to create value for shareholders and stakeholders? Part III outlines a process and a set of tools that managers can use to pursue the financial bottom line while effectively addressing social and environmental issues that are important to the company's future. The process and tools are designed to build agreement among such diverse constituencies as business unit heads and EH&S managers and thus enable companies to create business value in ways that are more robust than those used in traditional shareholder strategies.

CHAPTER TEN

Introduction to the Tool Kit

THIS CHAPTER introduces a tool kit to help business managers implement strategies for creating sustainable value. It covers the following key points:

- The concept of sustainable value
- Reframing business value to include stakeholders
- Rethinking stakeholders and their relationship to business
- The organization of the tool kit

The Concept of Sustainable Value

The core concept behind the frameworks and tools is that the financial value created by a business is always associated with a stakeholder value that can be either positive or negative. Positive stakeholder value is created when a business adds to the capital or well being of the individuals and constituencies it impacts. Negative stakeholder value is created when a business reduces their capital or undermines their well being.[1]

We can illustrate the difference between creating negative stakeholder value and creating positive stakeholder value by using the example of an aggregates company operating in a relatively dirty extractive industry:

- *The negative stakeholder value case:* The aggregates company operates stone quarries in ways that negatively affect the local community and ecologies through dust and noise pollution and poorly restored spent quarry lands. It does only what is required by law. There is little or no communication or coordination with the local community and NGOs.

• *The positive stakeholder value case:* The company operates stone quarries with standards for dust and noise control that are *beyond compliance* levels. It restores and rehabilitates spent quarry lands through reforesting and through reintroducing plant and animal species according to a plan codesigned with the local community.

In the positive stakeholder value case, the aggregates company benefits from more favorable permitting terms (faster permit approvals for extensions, permits of longer duration), reduced risk of community opposition to quarrying activities, and higher land values once the spent quarry site is sold. All these benefits translate directly into bottom-line profitability.

In every industry and sector, for every product or service, a range of stakeholders is impacted by a business's activities at multiple points along the value chain and thereby contributes to the company's profit opportunities or threats. Consider, for example, a company that makes industrial business-to-business products such as chemical dyes sold to the textile industry. In this company's production process, wastewater and auxiliary chemical residues are an economic and an environmental cost. Various stakeholder groups are impacted differently by environmental performance improvements to the process, but all are affected. The textile producer who purchases the dye values lower environmental clean-up costs and higher efficiency in the dye application process. The end customer values improved color uniformity; local communities value cleaner site operations; employees value a less toxic work environment; and investors and NGOs may value a smaller environmental footprint.

Stakeholder value may be a more obvious factor for companies such as Patagonia or The Body Shop, whose business-to-consumer products have a clear social or environmental dimension. Outdoors people and consumers of natural skin and hair products may be predisposed to pay more for positive social and environmental attributes in the products they buy.

Yet stakeholder value as a business proposition applies equally to business-to-consumer products that are by nature socially and environmentally damaging. Consider the automobile in its gas-guzzling sport-utility vehicle (SUV) embodiment compared to hybrid gas-electric or fuel-cell cars. Hybrid vehicles still create a negative impact on the environment, but compared to existing automotive technology they offer significant environmental and social benefits. These benefits—natural resource conservation, less air and noise pollution, and improved safety—are valued by a range of stakeholders at multiple points along the value chain. Such benefits then translate into business value for the industry leaders. (For anyone who doubts the imminent arrival of hybrid cars into the automotive mainstream, consider that in late 2002, GM announced it would offer hybrid power in five models by 2007, and Toyota announced that a broad range of its vehicles would be based on the hybrid platform by 2012.[2])

Finally, stakeholder value as a business proposition is increasingly important in services such as retail banking (see Chapter 8) and insurance companies (for example, AVIVA plc). In many cases, customers have recently demonstrated increased willingness to pay more for social and environmental performance.

Reframing Business Value to Include Stakeholders

In a wide range of industries, stakeholders are proving to be key drivers of business value. Traditionally, business has overlooked stakeholders in this role, preferring to rely heavily on ownership rights and access to resources as key determinants of its wealth-generating capacity. The problem of value creation now requires reframing in a way that goes beyond issues of access to capital, labor, technology, and location.

In 1980, Michael Porter's *Competitive Strategy: Techniques for Analyzing Industries and Competitors* helped shift the meaning of business value away from ownership rights and resource access and toward industry structure. Value creation (or destruction) came to be seen in terms of the threat of new entrants and substitute products, negotiating power with buyers and suppliers, and industry rivalry. Now the need is to expand the value-creating universe further to include an even broader array of stakeholders who contribute to the wealth-creating capabilities of a company. The concept of sustainable value expands the value-creating universe to include all key stakeholders.

The next section provides a vivid illustration of expanding value for the automotive industry. According to a 1999 report by the Union of Concerned Scientists, the use of personal vehicles is one of the most environmentally damaging activities in the world. It is only natural that companies offering a way to reduce the automobile's negative impacts on society and the environment, in an economical way, should find financial rewards. Although the transition to "clean and green" personal transportation is still in its early stages, the business case for it is instructive.

Creating Sustainable Value: Fuel-Cell Vehicles

A company's sustainable value depends on its ability to meet its customers' needs profitably while satisfying social expectations. For any of the leading companies in the car and truck industry today, senior managers in charge of running the business might reasonably conclude that they are doing a good job on both fronts: their products move their customers and their families, haul materials, and provide other personal mobility solutions safely and efficiently, thereby greatly benefiting society. Although not everyone would agree, a large majority of people in the world might support this view. Indeed, the record is impressive, whether measured in terms of improvements in fuel efficiency and safety, in comfort and road performance, or in percentage of junked automotive parts that can be recycled.

But when those same managers look 20 years into the future, a different picture emerges. Stakeholder impacts loom darkly on the horizon, and the promise of incremental improvements in technology does nothing to dispel the managers' worry. Consider what we know about how internal combustion engine (ICE) cars and trucks impact society and the environment—and then project 20 years forward, to a time when an expected 300 million additional vehicles are expected to be on the world's roads, reaching as many as 1.1 billion vehicles in total.

Negative stakeholder impacts begin with the relatively low energy efficiency (about 25 percent) of the ICE itself. Additional negative impacts are the result of a chassis design that combines the ICE with predominantly mechanical systems for steering, braking, and throttling. Cars typically weighing 3,000 to 4,000 pounds are designed to move four persons or fewer, contributing to energy inefficiency as well as to safety risks, noise, and urban congestion.[3]

For the industry as a whole, the manufacture and use of its products translates into the following environmental and social impacts:

- Degradation of ecosystems resulting from ozone-depleting releases; emissions of global warming gases such as carbon dioxide, carbon monoxide, and nitrogen oxides; and other chemical releases to the air.
- Solid waste and water contamination generated in the manufacture of steel, batteries, paints, plastics, lubricants, and other materials.
- Safety risks and noise emissions from heavy, mechanically complex vehicle designs.
- Degradation of public health and quality of life.
- Unsustainable resource use. The automotive sector is a significant contributor to the depletion of fossil fuels, consuming between one-third and one-half of the world's oil when the manufacturing process is included.

By contrast, hydrogen fuel-cell cars and trucks are twice as energy efficient as their ICE counterparts and emit nothing worse than water vapor. Although it takes energy to extract hydrogen from sources such as oil or natural gas, the fuel cell's high efficiency more than compensates for the energy required to accomplish the extraction. And eventually, the energy required to produce the hydrogen for fuel cells could come from renewable sources such as biomass, hydroelectricity, solar, wind, or geothermal energy.

When integrated with drive-by-wire technology, cars and trucks can be designed to be much lighter. The design has fewer constraints because a mechanical drivetrain is no longer needed. The space and weight freed up contribute to a potentially safer, more comfortable, more personalized, less expensive vehicle. In the GM conception, drive-by-wire fuel-cell vehicles (called Hy-wire, for hydrogen-by-wire) consist of an integrated skateboardlike chassis containing the fuel cell, electric drive motor, hydrogen storage tanks, electronic controls, heat exchangers, and braking and steering systems. The vehicle's body sits on top of the chassis, fitted together much like plug-and-play computer components. A simple visit to the dealer could enable the owner to pop up the existing body—say, a sports sedan—and replace it with another body such as a minivan, while keeping the same chassis. From the consumer's perspective, it's somewhat analogous to being able to switch the bezels on a Swatch: you get several possible models with one base unit.

The potential impact of fuel cell and drive-by-wire technological innovations on shareholder and stakeholder value is shown in Figure 10-1. Business value includes stakeholder value as a factor of performance. A conventional ICE-based product creates relatively moderate shareholder value[4] while eroding stakeholder value for the reasons just discussed. The fuel-cell product has a clear positive impact on stakeholder value and has the potential to raise shareholder value—although, as GM CEO Rick Wagoner has said, the economics of fuel-cell vehicles are still unclear. The added benefits of drive-by-wire designs could further improve both stakeholder and shareholder value.

Although the financial returns of mass-producing drive-by-wire fuel-cell vehicles remain unproved, we can discern the logic of increasing shareholder value from improved stakeholder value. Consumers who value the clean emissions, fuel efficiency, safety, comfort, and personalized designs of such vehicles will eventually pay more for them as the costs of air pollution and environmental degradation rise. The higher starting torque also provides a classic performance benefit: faster acceleration from a stop. Even though the full range of benefits is not yet available, early indicators of hybrid sales show faster than expected growth (see, for example, "Hybrid Cars Zip Off Lots," a Reuters newswire story by Timothy Gardner, August 19, 2001).

Vehicle manufacturers will also benefit from materials savings and

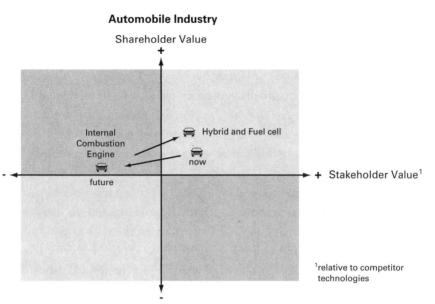

Figure 10-1. Automobile Industry Innovations

the lower capital intensity inherent in the greater design freedom afforded by the drive-by-wire and stackable fuel-cell technologies. Modular design could lower development costs through economies of scale of the base chassis models required to fit multiple body types. Having a smaller variety of components—such as can be achieved with fuel-cell stacks that can be scaled up or down—will further reduce costs.

Shareholder value will be created for those companies that succeed in shaping the automobile industry's rules of the game in their favor or who are better prepared for a sudden shift in consumer or regulatory requirements. Should there be a rapid transition to ultra-low-emission vehicles (ULEVs) or hybrid or fuel-cell vehicles, car manufacturers that achieve a cost advantage in any of these technologies may find that they now have a significant new competitive advantage. One analyst talks about Toyota's "raising the bar for the industry in the emerging environmental vehicle field."[5] Raising the bar for the new technologies translates into competitive barriers to entry—an important traditional source of shareholder value.

Two of the industry leaders who are betting big on the win-win of the new technology are General Motors and Toyota. While other automobile companies are currently outsourcing fuel-cell technologies to companies such as Ballard or United Technology Corporation, these two companies already have their own proprietary fuel-cell technologies.[6] GM's concept, called AUTOnomy, made a debut at the Paris auto show in September 2002, using the skateboard-type chassis design. GM is also planning to offer hybrid power in various stages of development for selected light trucks and SUVs within a few years. A hybrid version of the Saturn VUE is expected as early as 2005—a much more mainstream vehicle than the current Honda Insight. Dennis Minano, former vice president of public policy and chief environmental officer at GM, told me in an early 2003 interview that, in his view, GM had learned a great deal about how to pioneer a new generation of vehicles. "There is an advantage to being first to market with a fuel-cell vehicle if it is also affordable and competitive in performance terms," he said. "A fuel-cell vehicle that offers the broad range of features corresponding to how people make everyday decisions about personal mobility will create value for customers, shareholders, and society."

Toyota has been in the hybrid market since 1997 with the Prius[7] and is now prototyping fuel-cell vehicles based on the Highland platform. As reported in *The Green Business Letter* in its December 2002 issue, Toyota is now transitioning to a new phase, "sort of in between early adopter and mainstream," according to Ed La Roque, Toyota's manager of national advanced technology vehicles. With 36,000 hybrid vehicles already sold (at a profit on each vehicle), together with a public commitment to have its entire product range based on hybrid technology by 2012, Toyota is well positioned to create sustainable value for its shareholders and stakeholders in the new century.

There are still considerable barriers to realizing the vision of shareholder and stakeholder value presented here for the car and truck industry. The problems of storing hydrogen safely onboard the vehicle and reworking the infrastructure to supply energy to fuel-cell vehicles remain critical to mainstream success. However, the outlook is now much improved.

Rethinking Stakeholders and Their Relationship to Business

Companies know how to measure performance in terms of shareholder value. They are not used to measuring performance along the stakeholder dimension. Yet stakeholders increasingly represent a potential source of hidden value or risk to the future of the business.

The reframing of value creation does not focus on stakeholder issues as ends in themselves. The purpose is not to pursue social and environmental causes independent of economic payback. Such would be the case if the company operated only along the vertical axis in Figure 10-2, as it would with philanthropy. Instead, reframing value creation serves to implement an integrated approach to more significant and sustained benefits for the company, as shown by the diagonal arrow.

Al "Chainsaw" Dunlop notoriously repudiated the rights of stakeholders, adding, "You are not in business to be liked. . . . If you want a friend get a dog. I'm not taking chances; I have two dogs." But in the minds of many business leaders, stakeholders have gone from having illegitimate claims on business value, to having a limited voice primarily focused on ensuring compliance, to being external actors that

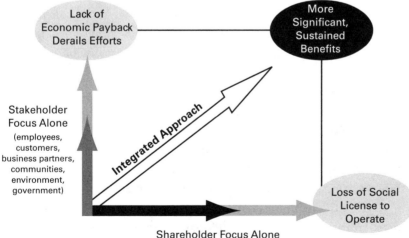

Figure 10-2. A Sustainable Value Approach Integrates Multiple Dimensions

businesses must tightly control, to being value-creating partners with whom the company can collaborate for mutual benefit. Today's mindset in business is hardly uniform, but it *is* changing. A review of the evolving perceptions of stakeholders helps give context to the tool kit and how it will be used.

Ann Svendsen, author of *The Stakeholder Strategy: Profiting from Collaborative Business Relationships* (1998), argues that 60 percent of corporate value is tied to such intangible assets as reputation, goodwill, employee know-how, and stakeholder trust. Cap Gemini Ernst & Young estimate that about 35 percent of investment portfolio decisions are driven by such intangibles as innovation, quality, customer relationships, leadership capability, alliances, brand reputation, and environmental performance.[8] Whatever the exact number, there is consensus that intangibles are a growing part of market capitalization and longevity. According to Svendsen, "Research now shows that companies that treat their employees, customers, suppliers and communities well are twice as likely to be around in the long term."

Svendsen makes a useful distinction between "stakeholder management" and "stakeholder collaboration." In the former type of relationship—fragmented, ad hoc, linked to short-term business goals, and focused on controlling outcomes—companies appear more business-focused yet paradoxically create lower value from their stakeholder engagements. They *manage* stakeholders in a hierarchical control model in which relative power determines whether the company or its stakeholders achieve their respective aims—when one wins, the other typically loses. In this light, Monsanto's attempt in the late 1990s to limit how (and when) farmers could use its genetically modified corn and Roundup Ready® soybean seeds could be seen as a failed attempt to manage consumer and environmental impacts by tightly controlling the outcomes.[9] This is not the view of stakeholders or of their relationship to a company implied in the sustainable value model.

In the sustainable value model, the focus is on building relationships, creating opportunities, and generating mutual benefits linked to long-term business goals. In collaborative stakeholder relations, there is an explicit coherence among economic, social, and environmental objectives.

STAKEHOLDERS IN THE SUSTAINABLE VALUE MODEL

Stakeholders are the individuals and constituencies that contribute voluntarily or involuntarily to the company's wealth-creating capacity; they are potential beneficiaries and/or risk bearers of the company's activities; as the term implies, they have a *stake* in the business.

The criteria for identifying significant stakeholders of a company are threefold:[*]

- They supply the resources that are critical to business success.
- They place something of value "at risk" (e.g., capital, their own welfare, their careers) that is directly affected by the fate of the business.
- They have sufficient power to affect the business performance either favorably or unfavorably.

It is the dynamic interaction and productive relationships with customers, employees, suppliers, investors, and other stakeholders that build a company's capacity to create future wealth.

[*] Thomas Kochan and Saul Rubenstein, "Toward a Stakeholder Theory of the Firm: The Saturn Partnership," 2000, *Organizational Science* 11(4): 373.

The locus of value in stakeholder relationships shifts from contracts (such as in legal compliance) and transactions (such as in philanthropic donations) to trust and cooperation. Companies are beginning to realize that conflict models that assume that increases in stakeholder value *are always offset by* reductions in shareholder value will lead to conflict and a draining of resources. On the other hand, win-win models based on pooling resources and a mind-set of cooperation can lead to shareholder value creation even when the company and its stakeholders appear to be on opposite sides of the fence.

When a company and NGOs cooperate, the former may gain access to technical expertise or community goodwill that it may not possess in-house, while the NGOs learn to be more efficient and bottom-line oriented. Weyerhaeuser's work to assess its forestry practices on the Tolt watershed in Washington State in the 1990s benefited from the company's relationship with representatives of the Tulalip Tribes, the Seattle Water Department, the Washington Environmental Council, and a number of other NGOs. The results were reported as "groundbreaking" in terms of fish savings, satisfying both Weyerhaeuser and some of its most outspoken critics.[10] Lafarge's cooperation with the WWF on climate change goals has helped it explore product mix alternatives, such as adding C-chemistry fly ash and slag to its traditional cement, at a faster rate than it might have done without the partnership, thus helping the company to reduce manufacturing costs and meet new greenhouse gas emission targets.

In today's complex world, a stakeholder perspective adds significant value to conventional strategic perspectives that focus primarily on resources and industry dynamics. Figure 10-3 summarizes some of the sources of shareholder value from collaborative stakeholder relationships.

In effect, rethinking stakeholders as potential sources of shareholder value is leading to a redefinition of the corporate entity. James Post, Lee Preston, and Sybille Sachs offer the following view of the corporation based on the collaborative stakeholder model:

> The corporation is an organization engaged in mobilizing resources for productive uses in order to create wealth and other benefits (and not to intentionally destroy wealth, increase risk, or cause harm) for its multiple constituents, or stakeholders.[11]

The tool kit is designed with this integrated, multiple stakeholder definition in mind—with one important qualifier: *the corporation's primary responsibility is still seen as delivering sustainable value to its shareholders.* To do so, however, companies are turning to stakeholders as a relatively untapped source of innovation and value creation—a key source of business advantage in the twenty-first century.

The Organization of the Tool Kit

Creating sustainable value through collaborative stakeholder relations requires specific financial, strategic, and measurement competencies

Stakeholders	Potential Sources of Shareholder Value
Investors	Access to socially responsible investor capital; potentially lower weighted average cost of capital (WACC)
Employees	Hiring and retention of talent Improved employee morale and productivity
Customers	Brand loyalty and reputation; goodwill and intangible value Collaboration in developing new products
Business partners	Access to strategic resources and capabilities
Unions	Improved labor relations and conflict resolution
Value chain associates	Cost-reducing/value-enhancing collaboration throughout value chain
Regulatory authorities	Validation of specific product/service quality levels. Lobbying regulations in company's favor. Increased flexibility with regulators
Governments	Favorable fiscal and industry-specific environmental and social policies
Local communities and citizens	Mutual support and accommodation. "License to operate." Reasonable treatment with respect to local taxes and service fees
Private organizations	Constructive collaboration with individual organizations and groups. Favorable public opinion environment. "License to operate"

Figure 10-3. Potential Sources of Shareholder Value by Stakeholder Group

that help integrate stakeholder impacts into the value delivery capability of a company. Based on our experience in working with Global 1000 companies, these competencies fall into *eight disciplines*, described in the following chapter.

We have structured the tool kit to help companies excel at sustainable value creation. The eight disciplines can also easily be fitted to change-management processes designed to help companies deal with discontinuous change. Relevant change-management processes are discussed in Chapter 12.

CHAPTER ELEVEN

The Eight Disciplines

COMPANIES ARE FINDING that specific strategic, financial, and measurement competencies are required to integrate stakeholder impacts into the value delivery capability of a company. Such managerial competencies as valuing investment opportunities using real options and determining changing customer preferences for a product are familiar to many executives. However, the application of these competencies to stakeholder impacts in a way that integrates those impacts into core business decisions remains unfamiliar territory in all but a handful of companies.

Figure 11-1 lists the eight disciplines that form the core competencies required to create sustainable value. All eight are essential to achieving the goal and must be considered as parts of a whole process.

The eight disciplines are integrated into a management process that executives can use in their organizations to discover and create sustainable value in a step-by-step approach, as shown in Figure 11-2. Six disciplines are organized into two subprocesses, *"Discover Value Opportunities"* and *"Create Value,"* with the seventh discipline serving as a feedback loop from one subprocess to the other. The eighth is a metadiscipline that uses the other seven to increase the organization's capacity to deliver sustainable value.

In our experience, mastery of these eight disciplines is critical to sustainable value creation. In particular, companies must be skilled at the two major components represented by the two boxes: discovering

Disciplines	Key Attributes
Understand current position	Understand where and how the company is creating or destroying shareholder and stakeholder value
Anticipate future expectations	Track key trends, identify emerging issues, and anticipate new stakeholder expectations
Set sustainable value goals	Establish a strategic intent and specific goals regarding how to create additional value for shareholders while reducing negative impacts and/or creating value for stakeholders
Design value-creation initiatives	Identify sources of value and design initiatives to capture shareholder and stakeholder value
Develop the business case	Build a compelling business case and obtain the resources needed to capture shareholder and stakeholder value
Capture the value	Undertake activities and implement initiatives to capture shareholder and stakeholder value
Validate results and capture learning	Measure progress; track and validate results in capturing shareholder and stakeholder value
Build sustainable value capacity	Develop the mind-set, capabilities, and skills needed to capture shareholder and stakeholder value

Figure 11-1. The Eight Disciplines of Sustainable Value

sustainable value opportunities and creating sustainable value. The competencies needed to identify the opportunities and those required to execute a plan to capture those opportunities are very different, and some companies have one set but not the other. A gap in either of these areas will thwart the intended result. Disciplines 7 and 8 are accelerators in the process of improving the other six and can make the difference between a company that has occasional successes in this area and a company that is a consistent leader.

Applying the Eight Disciplines

The scale at which a company uses the disciplines can vary widely—in some companies, the effort may start with a single initiative; in other cases, a company will use the disciplines in a specific business unit; in still others, the disciplines may be used company-wide. Scale is a much less important predictor of success than the inclusion of all the disciplines.

Companies can also start with any one of the eight disciplines as long as all eight are eventually included. The reality of large, complex orga-

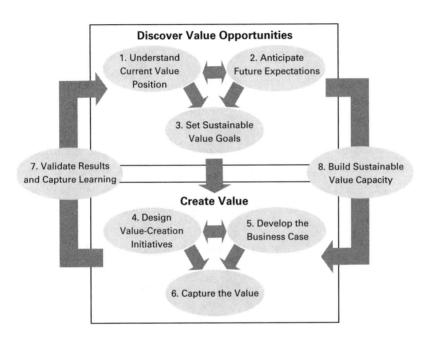

Figure 11-2. The Eight Disciplines of Sustainable Value

(1) Establish a baseline *value assessment* of business activities, including the value created or destroyed for key stakeholders. (2) Create a shared picture of future shareholders and stakeholder expectations and what this means in terms of business opportunities and risks. (3) Set a strategic intent and define goals for creating shareholder value while reducing negative impacts and/or creating value for stakeholders. (4) Design actions and initiatives with direct line management involvement. (5) Develop a financially rigorous business case for the initiatives that includes the resources required and the proposed payback. (6) Implement the initiatives to capture the value. (7) Validate the results and capture learnings. (8) Throughout the process, build organizational capabilities and skills needed to assess and capture sustainable value.

nizations is that the process of sustainable value creation is likely to be messy and opportunistic in the order of steps undertaken.

Consider the example of a specialty chemical manufacturer supplying dyestuffs to the textile industry for coloring cotton and rayon fiber. This company may not have a carefully thought out plan for creating sustainable value. It may not have—or even wish to have—a baseline assessment of its existing stakeholder impacts. In fact, it may be defensive about these performance areas, and senior management may oppose any efforts to include stakeholder issues.

Sustainable value creation in this company might begin with the design of a particular value creation initiative (Discipline 4). A company R&D team develops a new molecule that increases quality (higher fixation rates, better color consistency) and lowers environmental impacts for textile customers by reducing their amounts of waste dye and auxiliary chemicals. In early market tests, increased market share and higher margins draw the attention of senior management to new and emerging customer procurement criteria (Discipline 2): textile companies are suddenly buying dyestuff on the basis of price, quality, *and* environmental impacts, in response to skyrocketing wastewater treatment costs. Furthermore, the customers of the chemical company's customers are beginning to purchase finished textile products using environmental and social performance criteria. The company's current position (Discipline 1) is then evaluated relative to the emerging market expectations of environmental and social performance.

With the momentum of a successful initiative that helps to prove the business case (Discipline 5) in a business unit of the company, corporate staff charged with EH&S affairs or sustainable development become involved. The early success with an environmentally advantageous dye molecule is followed by further corporate-level efforts that engage the larger organization in developing a sustainable value intent and specific strategic goals for the company as a whole (Discipline 3). A cross-functional "sustainable value championship team," in partnership with business unit heads, is then charged with capturing sustainable value (Discipline 6) through additional products and services based on environmental or social attributes. The CFO organization is closely involved in measuring progress and validating results (Discipline 7). Once there are visible financial results, the board invests in building sustainable value capacity in diverse parts of the organization (Discipline 8). It is at this point that the company truly begins to transform itself into a socially and environmentally sustainable organization.

The eight disciplines, as a cohesive set of competencies, provide the best and most rigorous chances of success in creating sustainable value. The remainder of the chapter examines each discipline, showing the key tools required and, in many cases, examples of one or more companies applying these tools.

Discipline 1: Understand the Current Position

Understanding the current position means being able to determine the value created or destroyed by your company (or business unit or function) for its shareholders *and* its stakeholders. This requires an assessment of the impacts of the business on its stakeholders and of how those impacts lead to value creation or destruction.

The shareholder/stakeholder value map is a central tool in this assessment step. As described in Figure 11-3, only companies operating in the upper right quadrant, which deliver value to their shareholders without transferring it from other stakeholders, have a truly sustainable business.

A quarrying company that creates above-average dust and noise in the local community and an electronics manufacturer with an above-average toxic release index are examples of companies that—relative to their peers—transfer value from stakeholders to shareholders. Such companies need to assess their negative social and environmental performance in order to quantify the value risks as measured by consumers, investors, employees, and other stakeholders who track such performance.

The assessment should also include the extent to which EH&S and sustainable development initiatives add value along both dimensions. What value do these initiatives create for shareholders and stakeholders? The job of these initiatives is to move the products, services, and activities of the company toward greater shareholder and stakeholder value. Only when EH&S and sustainable development initiatives

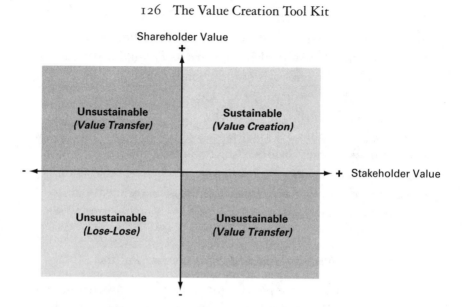

Figure 11-3. The Shareholder/Stakeholder Value Map
Discipline 1 Framework: Sustainable value is created when a company delivers value to shareholders without transferring it from other stakeholders.

- When value is created for stakeholders as well as shareholders (upper right quadrant), these stakeholders represent a potential source of hidden value.
- When value is transferred from stakeholders to shareholders (upper left quadrant), the stakeholders represent a risk to the future of the business.
- When value is transferred from shareholders to stakeholders (bottom right), the company incurs a fiduciary liability to its shareholders.
- When value is destroyed for both shareholders and stakeholders (bottom left), a lose-lose situation results.

are perceived as value contributors will they be effectively integrated into the business.

Companies can place their businesses (by product, process, business unit, or geographic area) on this map once they have an understanding of shareholder performance and stakeholder performance for each case. This map is particularly useful in tracking changes over time and in comparing business options. The following five examples illustrate real cases of value creation or destruction using the map.

Case Example 1: the aggregates industry

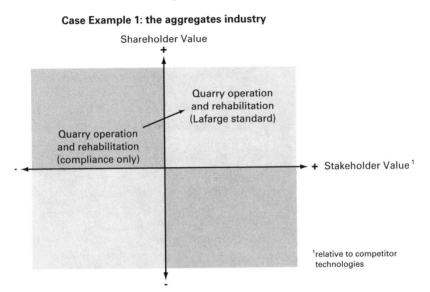

Quarries create dust, noise, and leave an unsightly landscape. Minimum compliance can result in "value destruction" for local communities and the natural environment. Lafarge is a global leader in the aggregates business. By exceeding minimum compliance in quarry operations and rehabilitation, Lafarge creates value for local stakeholders, leading to potentially new sources of profit.

Case Example 2: the chemical industry

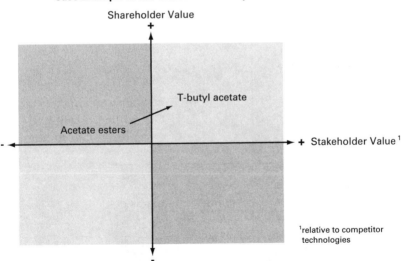

Acetate esters (mostly ethyl based) are solvents used in paints, inks, and other coatings. Already a low margin business, their classification as Volatile Organic Compounds (VOCs) poses hidden risks. Newly created T-butyl acetates offer the same performance and are VOC exempt, allowing price differentiation.

Figure 11-4. Assessing Your Company's Impact on Stakeholders and Shareholders

Case Example 3: the automobile industry

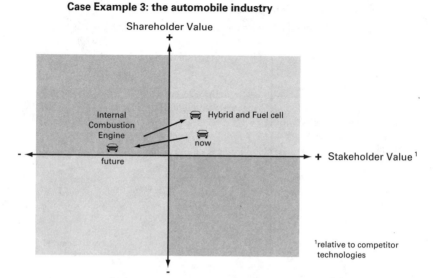

The personal mobility, fuel efficiency, safety, recyclability, and low cost of today's cars create economic and societal value, but its CO_2, CO, N_2O emissions, solid waste, and urban congestion will sharply reduce societal value in the future. Hybrid and fuel cell technologies may partly reverse these negative impacts.

Case Example 4: genetically engineered crops

Shareholder Value
+

Aventis Starlink

-          + Stakeholder Value

€1 billion loss

-

Starlink is genetically modified corn approved in 1998 for animal feed. Following contamination of corn crops for human consumption, Aventis was forced into buy-back programs costing it €1 billion by 2001, when it sold its Crop Sciences division to Bayer. The liability still remains with Aventis.

Figure 11-4, *continued.*

Case Example 5: the pulp and paper industry

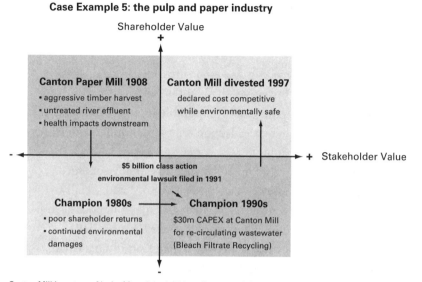

Shareholder Value

Canton Paper Mill 1908
- aggressive timber harvest
- untreated river effluent
- health impacts downstream

Canton Mill divested 1997
declared cost competitive
while environmentally safe

Stakeholder Value

$5 billion class action
environmental lawsuit filed in 1991

Champion 1980s ➝ **Champion 1990s**
- poor shareholder returns
- continued environmental
  damages

$30m CAPEX at Canton Mill
for re-circulating wastewater
(Bleach Filtrate Recycling)

Canton Mill is a story of lack of foresight. Initial environmental damages became liabilities after the US EPA legislated regulations and social awareness increased. As margins declined in a consolidating industry, owner Champion attempted to correct the problem, too late to avoid a $5 billion lawsuit. Canton Mill was then divested.

Figure 11-4, *continued.*

ASSESSING STAKEHOLDER IMPACTS

To assess their stakeholder impacts, companies begin with data from internal management systems such as Six Sigma,[1] compliance-based regulatory measures, and direct stakeholder input. Direct dialogue with stakeholders can take place in a variety of forums, such as community advisory panels. These sources of information should be tailored to a company's specific circumstances. They provide a baseline for the company's social and environmental performance.

These tools are usually not sufficient, however. To gauge market expectations of stakeholder performance and to determine what may be missing in an internal/compliance perspective, leading companies increasingly turn to stakeholder performance standards that offer the same rigor and objectivity as financial standards. Like financial standards, they may be subject to interpretation (and to misrepresentation), but they are converging to a global market metric for what it means to create or destroy value (see Chapter 3 for a more in-depth treatment of this subject). The main kinds of external performance indicators of stakeholder value are listed below. More detail on the first two categories is provided in the appendix.

- *Global reporting frameworks and performance standards,* such as the Global Reporting Initiative, the UN Global Compact, the Sullivan Principles, the Caux Roundtable indicators, the OECD Guidelines, and other agreed-upon reporting standards to which major global companies have become signatories
- *The capital markets,* represented by investment advisors such as INNOVEST or asset managers such as SAM and socially responsible investment rating agencies such as Total Social Impact or KLD in the United States, Core Ratings (France), SIRI (Australia), Pensions Investment Research Consultants (PIRC) (United Kingdom), Avanzi (Italy), Caring Company (Sweden), CentreInfo (Switzerland), FED (Spain), Jantzi (Canada), Scoris (Germany), and Triodos (Netherlands), among others
- *Industry measures,* such as those produced by Global Environmental Management Initiative (GEMI), the American Chemistry Council and its Responsible Care program, the Sustainable Forestry Initiative (SFI), the American Textile Manufacturers Institute (ATMI), and other industry initiatives

These external standards provide a degree of objectivity that is often missing in internal management systems or direct dialogue with stakeholder groups. The capital markets in particular offer a wisdom that stems from serving fund managers in search of shareholder value. The INNOVEST performance measures, for example, are designed with no overt social and environmental advocacy, no bias from any one individual or company, and a low likelihood of any single NGO overly influencing the metrics used. INNOVEST employs sophisticated econometric modeling to determine which environmental and sustainability measures are statistically correlated with financial performance. With about 60 performance measures tailored for each sector it studies, INNOVEST provides a much needed degree of objectivity and specificity to stakeholder value. In the automobile sector, for example,

INNOVEST evaluates the major automobile manufacturers using indicators such as CAFÉ standards, percentage cars versus light trucks, recyclability of the vehicles, ISO14001 compliance, the number of hybrid and fuel cell projects, and whether the company uses environmental performance factors in compensating its executives.

Of course, these external standards can (and should) be used in concert with one or more internal systems of measures. The converging sources of information on stakeholder value and how it is measured are shown in Figure 11-5.

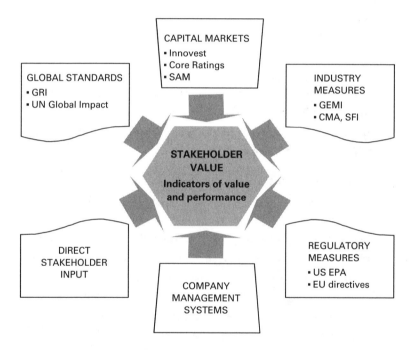

Figure 11-5. Stakeholder Metrics Are Identified

The challenge for companies is to develop a balanced process for determining what is important for their stakeholders. There is no one-size-fits-all approach, and stakeholder value is therefore best assessed using a tailored set of measures that fit the company's unique business situation and circumstances.

Here are some of the aspects to look for in assessing stakeholder impacts:

1. Severity and types of impacts
   a. Environmental (water, air, land quality, natural resources, food supplies, climate change, ecosystems and biodiversity)
   b. Social (wages, communities, political, employee safety, non-discrimination, cultural)
   c. Customers, suppliers, business partners
2. Location of impacts
3. Implications of impacts
   a. Business (fines, business risks, reputation)
   b. Ethical standards
4. Causes of impacts (policies, practices, processes, products)
5. Business opportunities and risks (wasted product, wasted inputs, unnecessary indirect costs)
6. Social challenges and opportunities within the operating environment and business scope

In determining the severity of stakeholder impacts, it is valuable for companies to consider the impacts of their products and activities *relative to absolute standards* and *relative to peers.* Absolute standards are those that meet the (generally scientific) tests for stakeholder well-being. For example, companies in the metal smelting and electroplating industries produce heavy-metal by-products that are highly toxic to human cells. These companies are unlikely to create anything but negative environmental impacts by the absolute standards of sustainability, but an individual company's performance can be far superior to the electroplating industry average, through the use of closed-loop processes and excellence in waste remediation practices. When stakeholder impacts are insufficient in an absolute sense but superior to peers, they can nevertheless translate into additional shareholder value.

Carrying out an effective stakeholder value assessment should result in the identification of stakeholder issues and impacts. The matrix in Figure 11-6 is a useful tool for this assessment. A company (or business unit or function) can use it to answer three questions: What are each stakeholder group's unique interests and issues in relation to our business activities? How do we affect this stakeholder group and create (or destroy) value for it? How does that stakeholder value translate into potential shareholder value? The reader can fill in the matrix for his or her business.

Completing this baseline assessment results in identification of the full range of impacts throughout the value chain, identification of the full range of stakeholder segments affected by those impacts, and a valuation of those impacts to understand where and how stakeholder value is being created or destroyed.

CHALLENGES

- Stakeholder value is more complex to measure and deal with than shareholder value. It requires judgment and is open to debate and conversation.
- Measuring stakeholder value is an emerging field having little uniformity within and across industries.

Stakeholders	Stakeholder Interests and Issues	Company Impacts on Stakeholder Value	Stakeholder Impacts on Shareholder Value
Communities		+ −	+ −
Environment		+ −	+ −
Government		+ −	+ −
Customers		+ −	+ −
Employees		+ −	+ −
Business Partners		+ −	+ −
Other		+ −	+ −

Figure 11-6. Matrix of Stakeholder Issues/Impacts

CRITICAL SUCCESS FACTORS

- Creating commitment to the concept of stakeholder value and a willingness to invest the time and energy to learn how to assess stakeholder value despite the challenges and pitfalls
- Keeping the analysis at the appropriate level of detail—deep enough to provide relevance and insight, but not so detailed as to cause endless debate and fruitless analysis
- Using the right measures—ones that are relevant to the industry and the real stakeholders yet reflect emerging performance standards (such as UN Global Compact, Sullivan Principles, INNOVEST)
- Segmenting stakeholder groups, linking stakeholder segments to the impacts, and then identifying those segments that require the most attention
- Assessing stakeholder value using both absolute standards and those that measure performance relative to peers

Discipline 2: Anticipate Future Expectations

Discipline 2 assesses probable future expectations of shareholders and stakeholders. It takes the baseline view of shareholder/stakeholder value created in Discipline 1 and asks, "What might change?" The purpose is to understand how shareholder and stakeholder expectations may evolve and what this means in terms of business opportunities and risks.

The use of "what-if" scenarios with quantified stakeholder impacts is key to a rigorous assessment of emerging trends. As described in my earlier book, *Large Scale Organizational Change*,[2]

> What-if scenarios are not undertaken as an exercise in prediction; they are part of creating a mindset that is open to radical change. If you are asking yourself what your company would do in case its future proves radically different from the past, it is probably already too late. Companies must integrate into their strategies a number of scenarios for radically alternative futures. Such envisioning of the future can remain fact based and issue driven, even if it represents a discontinuity with the past and present. . . . The syndrome of compiling quarterly reports and annual budgets can be

extremely limiting to a company's ability to adapt to fundamental change. Although these short-term exercises are efficient and necessary for a host of reasons, they must not allow senior management to privilege the short term at the cost of sustainability by optimizing existing structures and processes in a world in which these structures and processes are becoming irrelevant.

Leading companies develop a process for managing stakeholder expectations and emerging issues to create strategic opportunities for their business. They include feedback from stakeholder interviews and a regular scanning of emerging issues that are used to challenge assumptions in each business unit. To anticipate threats and opportunities, two types of scenarios are particularly important:

1. *High-probability, long-term, high-impact scenarios* drive thinking about major strategic shifts that demand deep changes in a company's capabilities. GM's look at the stakeholder issues surrounding the internal combustion engine 20 years into the future is such a scenario. In the face of such a long-term—but likely—future, an auto manufacturer that identifies its core competence with the internal combustion engine is increasingly at risk, and the investments required to shift to a new knowledge base are not trivial and cannot be made overnight. The risks to shareholder value for the late movers, and the potential opportunities for early movers, become clear through this discipline.

2. *Low-probability, short-term, high-impact scenarios* are also a priority. For a company such as Lafarge, with CO_2-intensive processes like cement manufacture, a sudden dramatic increase in the impact of climate change is such a scenario. In discussions with the head of environmental affairs at Lafarge in early 2003, CO_2 was identified as consuming "more than half" of the company's attention on sustainability issues. A review of the potential risks and opportunities of this scenario might lead the company to take real options on research into alternative building materials, in order to be positioned to sustain shareholder value in the event of a rapid shift to a more climate-constrained world.[4]

The key steps in the scenario process are

- Agree to relevant scenarios for this examination (scenarios A, B, C, and so forth). Use both issue life-cycle analysis and issue vulnerability analysis.
- Assess how future expectations will differ from current expectations for each key stakeholder segment under each scenario.
- Determine the implications of current and emerging issues. Use the matrix of stakeholder issues/impacts from Discipline 1 (see Figure 11-6) to assess the change.
- Identify and rank opportunities and threats.

These key steps are shown in Figure 11-7.

Based on filling out the stakeholder issues/impact matrix (from Discipline 1), the starting point for scenario building is in areas where the company significantly impacts the stakeholders and in areas where the stakeholders significantly impact the company. From these scenarios,

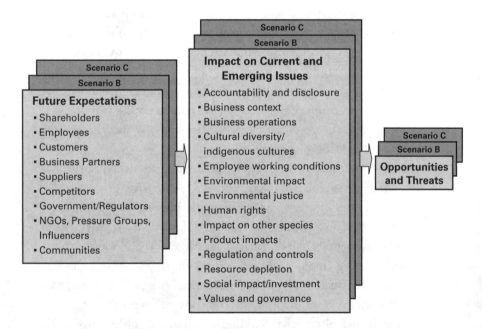

Figure 11-7. Creating Stakeholder Scenarios to Identify Future Opportunities and Threats

companies can assess emerging issues, prioritize actions, and develop contingent action plans.

In the case of the automobile industry, significant stakeholder impacts exist for safety, air emissions, solid waste and water contamination in the manufacturing process, public health and quality of life, and unsustainable resource use related to fossil fuels. In the 2003–2005 period, these impacts are not immediate risks to automobile companies. In the 2020–2030 period, however, the value at risk is much higher. The fuel-cell programs at GM and Toyota reflect contingent action plans based on alternative futures in which the internal combustion engine simply cannot deliver the social and environmental benefits that stakeholders will come to expect as a minimum to grant this industry a continued license to operate.

The last 30 years of regulatory and technological change in the automobile industry are instructive in this regard. Consumer and government concern with safety, fuel efficiency, and waste helped to drive environmental regulations and safety rules, leading to innovations in bumpers, safety constraints, catalytic converters, parts recyclability, and fuel-efficient engines. Future consumer and government concern about greenhouse gases, fossil-fuel dependence, and solid waste and water contamination are likely to drive radical innovations that will reshape personal transportation as we know it. Companies that position themselves to take advantage of such evolving stakeholder expectations will create value above the industry average (as the Japanese did in the 1970s in the U.S. market).

The outcome of Discipline 2 is a set of prioritized emerging issues and their implications for the business. The greatest potential for sustainable value creation lies in going beyond the known solution set. Engaging stakeholders can unlock hidden value and generate otherwise missed opportunities (new materials, processes, products, markets, rules of the game).

CHALLENGES

- Avoiding the fear that engaging stakeholders will open a Pandora's box. Companies such as Dow Chemical and Intel, with high potential risks, have successfully established stakeholder dialogue forums to identify and track emerging issues. Doing so has, if anything, decreased stakeholder resistance, rather than increasing it as they initially feared it would. Yet the initial fear of opening a Pandora's box of stakeholder issues is often present in such cases.

- Thinking outside the box and not just extrapolating trends from the past.
- Avoiding the tendency to see the company's impacts in a fragmented and unsystematic way. Seeing the complex interrelationships and potential reinforcing or feedback loops that can create risks or opportunities.
- Remaining practical.

CRITICAL SUCCESS FACTORS

- External listening to a broad range of information sources about emerging issues
- Creating focused, meaningful scenarios with quantified stakeholder impacts
- Including low-probability, high-impact trends and events

Discipline 3: Set Sustainable Value Goals

Discipline 3 establishes a vision and goals for how to create additional value for shareholders while reducing negative impacts and/or creating value for other stakeholders. Goals are mapped based on an identification of the products or activities that are negatively impacting shareholder/stakeholder value and that represent significant future risks given probable market and social expectations. They are also mapped based on significant future opportunities for value creation.

At the heart of this inquiry is greater awareness of the possibilities for creating environmental and social value throughout the value chain. Such an inquiry requires a creative vision for profitably meeting the needs of customers while creating social benefits. New value can be created in many ways, including better management of risks and reputation, reduction of waste, redesign of products to serve customers better while reducing safety hazards and harm to the environment, development of new businesses that contribute to improving social and environmental performance, and construction of a brand identity around corporate responsibility themes.

There are two key tools in this discipline. The first is the six levels of strategic focus. It helps a company to identify where sustainable value can be created. It makes it possible to choose from a broader range of strategic options than is usually the case in EH&S and sustainable development initiatives. The second tool is the sustainable value intent. Like the strategic intent used in classic visioning exercises for discontinuous change, the sustainable value intent gives voice to the aspirations of the company's leadership (or to the vision of one or more sustainable value champions in the organization). Here the resulting intent integrates stakeholder value and shareholder value into the vision of a desirable future for the business.

The Six Levels of Strategic Focus

The six levels of strategic focus shown in Figure 11-8 constitute an important tool for identifying value creation. You may recall how these foci were applied in the case of Bulmers, but here they are presented in general terms as they apply to virtually every company.

Many companies have made great strides in risk mitigation (level 1) and process cost reduction (level 2) through eliminating waste and improving energy efficiencies. Relatively few have focused on top-line growth based on product or brand differentiation (levels 3 and 5). Even fewer have used stakeholder value creation as a way to drive new markets and business context change (levels 4 and 6).

Yet the number of cases of green product or brand differentiation may be larger than is commonly believed. They range from mainstream examples such as United Parcel Service's bleach-free, 80 percent post-consumer recycled, reusable letter-size envelopes to niche examples such as Tokyo-based Triumph International Overseas Ltd.'s line of brassieres made from recycled plastic bottles. They include industrial business-to-business products such as environmentally friendly dyes sold to the textile industry; consumer products such as organic foods that avoid the use

Strategic Focus   **Sources of Value**

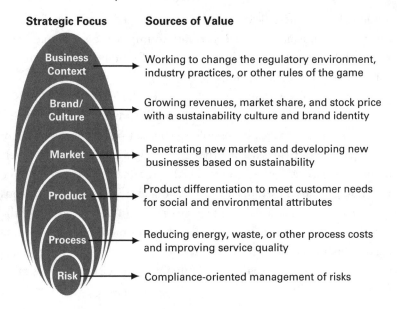

Business Context → Working to change the regulatory environment, industry practices, or other rules of the game

Brand/ Culture → Growing revenues, market share, and stock price with a sustainability culture and brand identity

Market → Penetrating new markets and developing new businesses based on sustainability

Product → Product differentiation to meet customer needs for social and environmental attributes

Process → Reducing energy, waste, or other process costs and improving service quality

Risk → Compliance-oriented management of risks

Figure 11-8. The Six Levels of Strategic Focus

of insecticides and antibiotics; and financial services such as full-service banking that screens loan applicants for ethical, social, and environmental performance.

Whatever level of strategic focus a company chooses, setting specific targets depends on creating a tangible vision of sustainable value. If it has done an effective job of assessing stakeholder impacts (Discipline 1) and future expectations (Discipline 2), the company may know that it needs to shift strategically, but it may not necessarily know how to formulate its vision and goals. That is the role of the sustainable value intent described here.

THE SUSTAINABLE VALUE INTENT

The sustainable value intent is simply a statement that is widely adopted throughout the organization. It expresses a particular desirable future that the company is committed to achieving and that combines superior shareholder value with stakeholder value. Like a traditional strategic intent, it sets ambitions greater than means; that is, it aims for targets that it doesn't know how to achieve given current capabilities.

These targets guide everything the company does. A sustainable value intent is valuable to organizations committed to sustainability because of its role in creating discontinuous change: it allows executives to design a future state that is informed by the past but is not an extension of it. In the vast majority of cases, a sustainable value creation strategy requires this kind of back-casting exercise. The outcome is an aligned senior leadership group. Or it can be an aligned middle-level team of sustainable value champions drawn from EH&S and line management or elsewhere in the organization. Whatever the circumstances of the company and its sector, an intent focused on sustainable value creation must include a stakeholder value dimension. BP in 1997 and Dupont in 2001 are examples of companies that were widely seen as environmental offenders 10 years earlier, yet developed strong strategic intents (think BP—Beyond Petroleum) to serve shareholders and the planet in a mutually reinforcing way.

In practice, the sustainable value intent has three key components:

1. *Vision:* A one-sentence declaration of an extraordinary future that the company is committed to achieving. Dupont's vision statement begins, "We, the people of Dupont, dedicate ourselves daily to the work of improving life on our planet."
2. *Values:* The shared principles and behaviors that guide how the company intends to conduct itself in pursuit of its vision. Dupont's principles state, "We will respect nature and living things, work safely, be gracious to one another and our partners, and each day we will leave for home with consciences clear and spirits soaring."
3. *Strategic objectives:* The concrete business goals that will allow the company to realize its vision and values. Dupont's sustainable value goals include the following four goals for 2010, supplementing existing financial goals:
   a. To derive 25 percent of revenues from nondepletable resources—up from 14 percent in 2002.
   b. To reduce global carbon-equivalent greenhouse gas emissions by 65 percent, using 1990 as the base year. The company has already surpassed this goal with a 68 percent reduction.
   c. To hold energy use flat, using 1990 as the base year.

d. To source 10 percent of the company's global energy use in the year 2010 from renewable resources.

The practical steps for creating the intent are based on my work in this area with several Fortune 1000 companies:

1. Grounding in Disciplines 1 and 2. The business context is defined in terms of shareholder and stakeholder value. The current state of the business and probable future expectations provide a shared understanding for the team involved.
2. Brainstorming. How would our company look in an extraordinary future? What would it be like around here?
   a. Speculating; generating elements of vision, values, and strategic objectives.
   b. Elements are left for at least a 12-hour period without evaluation, prioritization, or selection.
2. Criteria selection. What criteria will we use to evaluate, prioritize, and select the elements? Selection of five to eight key benchmarks specific to the company.
   a. Shareholder value criteria
   b. Stakeholder value criteria
3. Synthesis and alignment of purpose.
   a. Work in groups on selecting elements.
   b. Check elements left out from the previous day.
   c. Group elements.
   d. Vote on formulating the sustainable value intent.
   e. Create alignment and recommendations to pass on to the senior leadership.

Discipline 3 is about developing a vision with specific targets to improve shareholder and stakeholder value. It draws on the stakeholder impact assessment of Discipline 1 and the understanding of emerging issues of Discipline 2 to map out value enhancement opportunities using both shareholder and stakeholder dimensions. These opportunities occur at multiple levels of value creation and include risk mitigation, process improvement, product redesign, new markets, enhanced brand reputation, and a more favorable business context.

The targets should typically focus on near-term value improvement—the "quick wins"—to gain adherence and buy-in from line managers and financial executives who may be skeptical or who may consider performance targets involving stakeholders to be a low priority. The targets should also be fixed in collaboration with line management (through cross-functional guiding coalitions or steering teams) so as not to be seen as EH&S affairs that somehow lie outside the core business.

The resulting targets can be mapped as suggested in Figure 11-9. In this illustration, the target for activity E offers the greatest potential for value creation and is likely to get rapid buy-in from the rest of the organization. The target for activity A may be a much harder sell: although it significantly reduces stakeholder value destruction, it does not create any visible improvement in shareholder value. Success in setting the target for A will depend on making the business case that reducing negative stakeholder impacts provides various hidden benefits for shareholders—benefits that the managers proposing the target will have to reveal and articulate in financial terms.

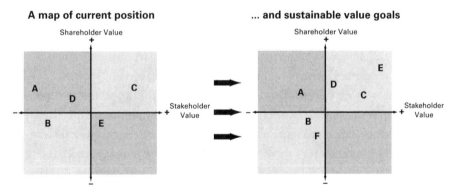

Figure 11-9. Setting Sustainable Value Goals for Activities A through E

CHALLENGES

- Getting support from senior management, ideally at the level of the CEO
- Getting the right people to work on goal setting

- Pursuing targets that may not have measurable cash-flow benefits today but either significantly reduce negative stakeholder impacts or create positive stakeholder value that could translate into shareholder value in the future

CRITICAL SUCCESS FACTORS

- A willingness to look at a wide range of ways in which business value can be created or destroyed. For example, thinking about environmental performance not only in terms of cost reduction and risk mitigation but also as a source of brand value and product differentiation.
- Greater awareness of the possibilities for creating environmental and social value throughout the value chain.
- Effectively using the insights and information from Disciplines 1 and 2 when setting the strategic intent and specific sustainable value targets.

Discipline 4: Design Value Creation Initiatives

The purpose of Discipline 4 is to design initiatives to meet the priority goals established through the previous disciplines. Another goal is to integrate stakeholder perspectives into existing initiatives such as Six Sigma, balanced scorecard, or supply-chain management.

The process benefits from cross-functional working teams and sponsorship by an executive steering committee to obtain the organizational buy-in and resources required at this stage. The sustainable value leaders will often call for one or more workshops that engage internal and external stakeholders as appropriate. The output is a completed initiative design and initiative implementation plan that has broad support inside the organization.

The key to Discipline 4 is establishing appropriate design criteria so that the initiatives address the six levels of strategic focus and the stakeholder sources of value identified in the previous discipline. Too often, EH&S or sustainable development initiatives focus only on risk mitigation or process cost reduction. Although these continue to be important sources of value creation for many companies, product differentiation, new markets, brand enhancement, and changing the rules of the game based on stakeholder performance represent a potential that is often left untapped.

The six levels of strategic focus for designing value creation initiatives are described here with illustrations and examples.

LEVEL 1: RISK MITIGATION — COMPLIANCE-ORIENTED MANAGEMENT OF RISKS

Many of the actions companies take to comply with government regulations and industry standards (such as Responsible Care in the chemicals industry) are seen as a financial burden: they are the necessary cost of doing business. Yet efficient risk mitigation strategies can create significant value to shareholders and stakeholders. They include the avoidance of penalties and fines, reduced legal fees, lower insurance premiums and/or product liability costs, reduced site remediation costs, and a lower probability of catastrophic events.

LEVEL 2: PROCESS COST REDUCTION — REDUCING ENERGY, WASTE, OR OTHER PROCESS COSTS AND IMPROVING SERVICE QUALITY

Process cost reductions are often one of the first stakeholder-oriented initiatives a company undertakes. Reducing environmental costs such as solid wastes, air emissions, or water runoff saves the company money while reducing environment, health, and safety impacts on local communities, employees, consumers, and other stakeholder groups. Process cost reductions can be addressed in the framework of existing operational efficiency initiatives such as Six Sigma and become an incremental extension of efficient resource use. Finally, efforts to reduce environmental process costs can provide the context for process innovation and reveal other opportunities for redesigning value-added activities or the products and services offered.

LEVEL 3: PRODUCT DIFFERENTIATION TO MEET CUSTOMER NEEDS FOR SOCIAL AND ENVIRONMENTAL ATTRIBUTES

The growing segment of consumers for whom social and environmental attributes are important decision criteria provides an opportunity for many companies to differentiate themselves on a dimension other than price or technical performance. The rapid growth of the cultural creatives segment of the population, now estimated by Paul Ray (see Chapter 5) at 50 million adults in the United States and 80 million in Europe, is fueling this third dimension of product offering. Bruce Piasecki of the AHC Group refers to this as the "social response" dimension and shows how companies such as Toyota are positioning themselves for industry leadership with environmentally differentiated products like the hybrid-based Prius.

LEVEL 4: MARKETS — PENETRATING NEW MARKETS AND DEVELOPING NEW BUSINESSES BASED ON SUSTAINABILITY

Technological innovation that creates stakeholder value increasingly opens up new markets. For example, Celanese AG has parlayed its expertise in plastic polymers to develop the first high-temperature membrane electrode assembly (MEA) for fuel cells suitable for use in cars, itself a new market driven by climate change–related concerns.

In other cases, developing an expertise in reducing stakeholder impacts or creating stakeholder value can open up a new line of business. For example, cement companies with high CO_2 emissions today face a liability. CO_2 emission caps, carbon taxes, plant shutdowns, and even asbestos-type class action lawsuits loom on the horizon. A cement company that is able to reduce its CO_2 emissions more cost efficiently than others has an opportunity to enter a new market: selling CO_2 credits.

LEVEL 5: BRAND AND CULTURE — GROWING REVENUES, MARKET SHARE, AND STOCK PRICE WITH A SUSTAINABILITY CULTURE AND BRAND IDENTITY

Patagonia, The Co-operative Bank, The Body Shop, and many midsize players are finding that a brand/culture based on creating stakeholder value is a source of competitive advantage. Whether mainstream play-

Strategic conditions	Patagonia outdoor equipment $225 million	Cargill-Dow packaging materials $600 million	Toyota automobiles $106 billion	Ciba specialty chemicals $6 billion	StarKist canned tuna $560 million	ARCO gasoline $12 billion
Differentiation focus	Social and environment activism	Polyactide polymer	Hybrid engines	Bi-reactive dyes	Dolphin-free tuna	Reformulated gasoline
Customer willingness to pay more						
Credible information about environmental and social performance						
Barrier to entry						

▨ = condition present   ▨ = condition partially present   ☐ = condition not present

Figure 11-10. Key Conditions in Product/Brand Differentiation
Key success factors in product and brand differentiation based on social and environmental attributes (levels 3 and 5). The above six companies have focused on product or brand differentiation based on social and environmental attributes. The table uses key strategic conditions for success first suggested by Harvard Business School professor Forest Reinhardt. The author is indebted to Professor Reinhardt's *Down to Earth: Applying Business Principles to Environmental Management* (Cambridge, Mass.: Harvard Business Press, 2000) for first suggesting the key strategic conditions for social response product differentiation.

ers can effectively position their brands and cultures in terms of stakeholder performance is yet to be demonstrated—although Toyota, Dupont, BP, and Shell are interesting, but still unconvincing, examples.

LEVEL 6: BUSINESS CONTEXT—WORKING TO CHANGE
THE REGULATORY ENVIRONMENT, BUSINESS PRACTICES,
AND INDUSTRY RULES OF THE GAME

At this level, companies attempt to shape in their favor the regulations, practices, and rules that govern how business can be conducted. A good example is the effort by cement companies and other CO_2 emitters to lobby for income tax offsets to eventual carbon taxes, thereby preserving the equity base of the industry. Individual companies that obtain an advantage in a particular stakeholder performance category may lobby legislators to impose harsh penalties in that category on the whole industry in anticipation of obtaining a new source of competitive advantage or creating a new barrier to entry.

Influencing the business context is not only about lobbying government. Increasing the overall stakeholder value in an industry can create goodwill for the entire industry or reduce negatives, as the Responsible Care program did for the chemical industry post-1990. Another example is the Pollution Prevention Partnership (3P) in the paper industry.

DEFINING CAPABILITY REQUIREMENTS

Once initiatives are selected and clear targets are set, the organization must assess the capabilities it will need. These are collective abilities of the organization required to capture and sustain value successfully. They cover a range of functions: customer service, stakeholder engagement, financing, human resources, marketing, operations, and product/service development. Example capabilities include

- Customer responsiveness
- Service integration
- New technology integration
- Design for environment
- Community engagement
- Serving developing markets.

Figure 11-11 is the visual representation of a tool for identifying capability surpluses and gaps by mapping current performance against the importance of capabilities for implementing a particular initiative.

"Needed to win" capabilities

- Are a key source of competitive advantage
- Are a source of clear distinction versus competitors
- Provide higher returns through excellent performance

"Needed to play" capabilities

- Are required to operate in the competitive marketplace

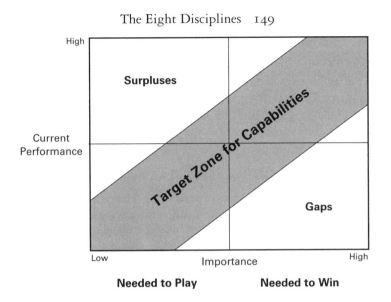

Figure 11-11. Assessing the Target Zone for Capabilities

- Are a foundation upon which "needed to win" capabilities are built
- Provide no competitive advantage through superior performance

The outcome of this discipline is a prioritized set of value creation initiatives that move the company toward the win-win quadrant of shareholder/stakeholder value, a prioritized set of capacity gaps, and actions for closing the gaps.

Discipline 4 leads to a completed initiative design and implementation plan. In the next step, establishing a rigorous business case for the initiative creates broad organizational support and provides the justification for implementation.

CHALLENGES

- Designing and getting buy-in for initiatives that do not have obvious payoffs. For example, human rights policies that go beyond minimal compliance requirements.
- Getting line management and financial staff to see EH&S and sustainable development initiatives as something other than a waste of time.
- Getting the resources or approval for investments for initiatives

before making the business case (Discipline 5). Conversely, not being able to make the business case until the value creation initiatives are approved.

- For initiatives at the business unit level, reluctance to push for context changes that create a disadvantage for the industry as a whole.

CRITICAL SUCCESS FACTORS

- Cross-functional teaming and sponsorship by an executive steering committee to obtain the organizational buy-in and resources required at this stage
- Partnering with line management
- Partnering with the CFO organization
- Working at all six levels of strategic focus (not just risk mitigation and cost reduction)
- Assessing the organizational capabilities needed to capture and sustain value successfully

Discipline 5: Develop the Business Case

Discipline 5 helps to build a compelling business case for the sustainable value initiatives and to obtain the resources and organizational support needed to implement them.

Once the priority initiatives have been identified, scoped, and designed (Discipline 4), it is time to quantify (where possible) the shareholder and stakeholder impacts in each case.

- Project the costs and benefits, considering the timing and complexity of implementation.
- Assign a monetary value, to the extent possible, of each initiative, including the impact of stakeholder value on shareholder value.
- Obtain input and buy-in from the line managers who will ultimately be accountable for delivering the results.

Here such innovative tools as real-options analysis and stakeholder diagnostics help to quantify the business value of specific social and environmental initiatives.

Value Drivers

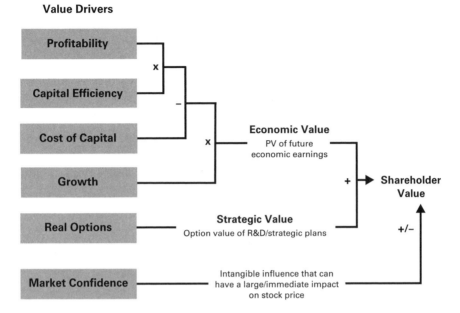

Figure 11-12. Opportunities must be assessed against their potential to create shareholder value

The financial framework relies on two tools that work together to quantify the business case for sustainable value initiatives. The first tool is the six levels of strategic focus presented in the previous sections (see Disciplines 3 and 4). The second tool is the six drivers of shareholder value presented here.

The six drivers of shareholder value (Figure 11-12) show the key ingredients of shareholder value. The top four value drivers in the left-hand column are the classic drivers of *economic value added (EVA)*. The remaining two drivers are *strategic value* and *market confidence*.

Strategic value assessed through real-options analysis is a powerful way to account for the *foresight* of management teams in creating opportunities and managing risks from emerging issues that might threaten shareholder value. In concept, real options are similar to financial options. Financial options are the right to buy a security at a set date in the future (exercise date) for a set price (strike price). On the exercise date, if the security is worth more than the strike price, then the holder of the option will exercise it and purchase the security. If the security is worth less than the strike price, the investor will not purchase the security.

Real options represent R&D programs, strategic plans, and other activities that position a company to take advantage of an opportunity by making additional investments at a future date. The additional investments represent the strike price of the real option. The underlying security is the future cash flow of the new business. The company will make the additional investments on the exercise date if, at that time, it appears that the business will be profitable. If, on the other hand, conditions are such that the business is unlikely to be successful, the company will save itself from having to make an unprofitable investment. Thus, the real option allows a company to manage future uncertainty through (1) delaying investment until more is known and (2) being ready to move quickly when the conditions are right.

Just as a financial option has value whether or not it turns out to be "in the money," a real option also contributes to shareholder value even if it is never exercised. The Black-Scholes formula for calculating the value of financial options can be used with real options as well.

The management team can use real options in a powerful way to pursue the corporate responsibility strategies described above. Given future uncertainties, some investments required to pursue these strategies many not be justifiable using EVA or discounted cash flows. Yet ignoring the uncertainties may leave a company vulnerable to future events. Real options provide a means of economic justification for strategic action as insurance or as a possible source of future competitive advantage.

In particular, real options enable companies to incorporate low-probability, high-impact scenarios into their value assessment, something that is very difficult to do using a pure EVA approach to valuation. For example, an oil company using real options could develop strategic plans and justify R&D and exploratory investments in alternative energy to position it to move quickly if global warming turns out to be more severe than anticipated.

Market confidence is an intangible influence that can have a large and immediate impact on share price. Of course, some portion of market confidence is driven by the overall state of the market and the industry and is not under the direct control of management. But to a significant degree, this factor is a reflection of management integrity. As recent events have shown, the absence of this integrity can undermine shareholder value more radically than any competitor's action or market fluctuation.

One of the best measures of a company's management integrity is its track record in stakeholder value creation. The investment research firm INNOVEST, as mentioned earlier, specializes in analyzing companies' environmental, social, and governance performance and the resulting impact on shareholder value. The firm finds a consistent correlation between stakeholder performance and sustained growth in shareholder value.

The six drivers of shareholder value can be combined with the six levels of strategic focus to create a sustainable value matrix. An example of a completed value matrix is provided in Figure 11-13, for a heavy-industry company that undertook to reduce CO_2 emissions beyond

CO_2 reduction example: Value Drivers

Levels of Strategic Focus	Strategic Options	Capital Efficiency	Cost of Capital	Growth	Real Options	Market Confidence
Business Context	Influence regulators to cost-effectively meet Kyoto targets					
Brand/Culture			Attraction of socially responsible investors			
Market				Sale of CO_2 credits		
Product					Research into new less-energy intensive products	
Process	Savings in fuel costs and in production costs	Fewer assets required for same level of production				CO_2 leadership is indicator of management quality
Risk	Avoid the costs and negative publicity of shareholder initiatives	Better capital investment decisions that include future carbon taxes and market values			Flexibility to move quickly if regulations are more severe than expected	

Figure 11-13. A value matrix identifies all sources of value

compliance requirements. By looking across all six levels of strategic focus and all six financial drivers, the company was able to articulate to its line management and shareholders why this environmental initiative was good for business. A quantified dollar impact was calculated for key sources of value.

Discipline 5 leads to the strategic and financial justification for the value creation initiatives. It is what creates cross-functional executive alignment regarding justification, next steps, and roles during implementation.

CHALLENGES

- Getting input and buy-in from line management and financial managers.
- Developing the business logic for the implications of stakeholder value for shareholder value. For example, why does rehabilitating an industrial site or greening a building beyond what is required by law create shareholder value rather than simply cost the company money.
- Getting cash data for EVA calculations.
- Calculating real options.
- Avoiding the perception that ethics is being monetized.

CRITICAL SUCCESS FACTORS

- Projecting the costs and benefits in a meaningful way, given the timing and complexity of implementation when multiple stakeholders are involved
- To the extent possible, assigning a monetary value for each initiative, including the impact of stakeholder value on shareholder value
- Obtaining input and buy-in from the line managers who will ultimately be accountable for delivering the results

Discipline 6: Capture the Value

Discipline 6 represents the ability to execute the value creation initiatives. It embeds social and environmental initiatives into the organization with cross-functional implementation teams. These teams often have the support of an executive steering committee or guiding coalition. This discipline requires the managers responsible for implementation to work collaboratively with stakeholders—including external stakeholders—in a way that guarantees transparency and learning. It requires the initiatives to be integrated into the management and accountability structures and processes. It establishes two-way communication mechanisms and action meetings to engage key stakeholders throughout the implementation process.

Stakeholder value is thus captured as part of how the core business value is delivered. For example, rather than a parallel Total Quality Environmental Management (TQEM) effort, environmental efficiencies are integrated into Six Sigma.

Discipline 6 requires stakeholder management and engagement as part of the normal course of business. It benefits from continual testing: piloting new ideas, developing short-term wins, and learning from successes and failures. The added complexity of multiple stakeholders makes the classic "golden rules" of leadership and management all the more relevant.

1. Leadership
    a. Happens at many levels
    b. Involves a guiding coalition or key influencers
    c. Uses internal and external communication to capture the imagination and provide inspiration
2. Management
    a. Implementation and governance structures effectively set priorities and include those with organizational responsibility.
    b. A process exists for managing the necessary details and the many commitments.
    c. New initiatives are integrated with Six Sigma and/or other key sources of value capture.
    d. Cross-functional implementation teams are used throughout.

Often, many of the best tools for Discipline 6 are those you already use, adapted to include stakeholder as well as shareholder perspectives. These might include Six Sigma, Total Quality Management (TQM), supply chain integration, customer management, and reengineering. These traditional business tools benefit from softer, culture-change approaches when new stakeholders and social or environmental issues are introduced. Culture-change approaches to implementing sustainable value initiatives often involve stakeholder surveys, focus groups, and advisory councils to help shape leadership development programs or culture-change programs focused on the mind-sets and behaviors of executives in the organization.

The approach should be to adopt the tools that your organization has already used successfully. Where gaps exist, managers should look to best-practice tools adapted to their particular situation.

CHALLENGES

- The hand-off between the designers and the implementers can be confusing because of the many stakeholders involved.
- Lack of senior level support.
- Turns into just one more initiative.
- Key level of line management is out of the loop.
- Green wall: inability to take actions together (EH&S, CFO, line management, stakeholders).
- Turns into a parallel management structure that undermines line management.
- People don't understand what it is about and do not get behind it.
- Stakeholder opportunities and risks are ignored or undermanaged.
- It takes too long to see results, so the organization loses interest.
- Getting the appropriate degree of involvement from stakeholders.

CRITICAL SUCCESS FACTORS

- Embedding social and environmental initiatives into the organization with cross-functional implementation teams and an executive steering committee
- Working collaboratively with stakeholders in a way that guarantees transparency and learning
- Integrating the initiatives into the management and accountability structures and processes

- Establishing two-way communication mechanisms and action meetings to engage key stakeholders throughout the implementation process

Discipline 7: Validate Results and Capture Learning

This discipline is the systematic results tracking and feedback loop that enables learning and improvement in the organization. The metrics used in Discipline 1 to establish a baseline assessment of shareholder and stakeholder value are used here to measure progress made. The components of this discipline include

- Regularly assessing actual progress in achieving targets defined in the business case.
- Holding learning-focused reviews of the initiatives to assess potential barriers to value realization and revise initiative approaches as needed.
- Reviewing many initiative results against the overall sustainable value goals and refining the goals as appropriate.
- In addition to tracking results, this process should capture lessons learned about the process of sustainable value creation in order to refine the organization's tools, processes, and frameworks, in particular regarding stakeholder dialogue, stakeholder value assessment, and business case development.

One of the biggest challenges in this discipline is integrating a broader set of stakeholder metrics into operations. If the company already uses a balanced scorecard approach to measurement, where economic stakeholders such as customers and supply chain partners are represented, then extending this scorecard to include social and environmental performance measures will be easier.

A critical success factor in this discipline is to engage the CFO organization in the process of broadening the metrics used to assess and report shareholder value, including strategic value (the option value of R&D and strategic plans). Another success factor is embedding stakeholder performance tracking and reporting in the line organizations.

CHALLENGES

- Tailoring the metrics to the business
- Integrating the stakeholder metrics into operations (extending the balanced scorecard approach to include social and environmental performance measures)

CRITICAL SUCCESS FACTORS

- Getting the CFO organization fully engaged
- Getting the CFO organization to broaden the metrics used to assess and report shareholder value (for example, to include strategic value and market confidence)
- Getting line management to work with EH&S and the CFO organization in tracking and reporting stakeholder performance
- Creating a learning culture and valuing effective learning conversations among all team members

Discipline 8: Build Sustainable Value Capacity

Discipline 8 is a metadiscipline focused on developing the mind-set and capabilities needed to embed a sustainable value perspective into the organization. It includes making changes to existing processes, such as those that determine how investments are approved. It also includes the creation of new processes for such tasks as stakeholder engagement and dialogue and new measurement systems, such as expanding a balanced scorecard to include stakeholder value metrics. Most important, it includes changes to people's mental models of the role and importance of stakeholders as a source of value creation. Achieving leadership in sustainable value creation demands a coherent, organized approach not only within each discipline but also across disciplines.

The outcome of this discipline is that the organization becomes skilled at each of the preceding seven disciplines. Discipline 8 promotes a new way of thinking about value creation, systematically bringing a stakeholder perspective into the firm. Every action and interaction supports a sustainable value approach to business.

The various competencies required to do this for each discipline are listed on the following page.

Building Sustainable Value Capacity for Discipline 1: Understand Current Value Position

- Frame the value creation problem to see stakeholders as opportunities rather than threats.
- Be willing to look at stakeholders as potential sources of business value.
- Broaden what managers consider to be the boundaries of business.
- Offer executive education on the business logic of sustainable value.
- Use systems thinking in assessing stakeholder impacts.

Building Sustainable Value Capacity for Discipline 2: Anticipate Future Expectations

- Commit to investing time and energy in exploration of trends and issues, and base the effort on the belief that such an exploration will be a source of value.
- Establish a regular process for scanning emerging issues.
- Strengthen the ability to recognize which issues are meaningful.
- Create a process for identifying low-probability, high-impact events. In scenario building, learn to detach from the business model that generated the company's success in the past.

Building Sustainable Value Capacity for Discipline 3: Set Sustainable Value Goals

- Look at different stakeholder groups, and what business benefits they bring, as a way to determine how to set targets and at what level.
- Set targets that stretch the organization (the strategic intent). Go beyond the known solution set.
- Get clear about individual and organizational core ideology.
- Look at top-line sources of value, particularly those shaping the business context and the regulatory environment.

Building Sustainable Value Capacity for Discipline 4:
Design Value Creation Initiatives

- Design products and initiatives with new principles such as those of *The Natural Step* or Bill McDonough and Michael Braungart's *Cradle-to-Cradle: Remaking the Way We Make Things.*
- Design with these new principles integrated into core business efforts such as Six Sigma. Expand Six Sigma to include the product design level.
- Get collaboration from value chain partners. Extend stakeholder value criteria to your value chain partners (education and shift of mind-set).

Building Sustainable Value Capacity for Discipline 5:
Develop the Business Case

- Simplify the analytics so that you can get beyond the number crunching and stay focused on the logic of sustainable value.
- Create cross-functional teaming. Develop a process for working across the functions, creating synergies rather than compromises.
- Strengthen the ability to project the uncertainties of a new business in financial terms.

Building Sustainable Value Capacity for Discipline 6:
Capture the Value

- Develop team practices for collaborative work. Build project management competence that includes external stakeholders.
- Walk the talk: in every aspect of implementation, demonstrate transparency and partnership with key stakeholders.
- Ensure that line management integrates the sustainable value initiatives into the business delivery system (and that they are not treated as parallel to the core business).
- Establish two-way communication mechanisms and action meetings to engage key stakeholders throughout the implementation process.

Building Sustainable Value Capacity for Discipline 7: Validate Results and Capture Learning

- Familiarize managers with the broad array of emerging stakeholder metrics. Learn about the stakeholder measures that are relevant to the specific sector and company circumstances.
- Focus on the measures of stakeholder value that are significant, out of the large number of possible impacts, indicators, and metrics.
- Link quantified stakeholder value to shareholder value in a way that is compelling to line and financial management.

Building Sustainable Value Capacity for Discipline 8

To a large extent, Discipline 8 focuses on the organizational process of achieving sustainable value, whereas the preceding seven disciplines focus on the goals to be achieved (baseline assessment, identification of emerging issues, target setting, and so forth). The next chapter develops the process aspects further and looks at sustainable value creation from the perspective of managing change.

CHAPTER TWELVE

Putting It All Together

THE EIGHT DISCIPLINES fit easily into the change management process shown in Figure 12-1. In many ways, it reflects a classic approach to discontinuous change. Peter Drucker suggested similar approaches as early as the 1960s.[1] Here this backbone of change management has been adapted to the specific challenges presented by multiple stakeholders and revised assumptions about business's role in society.

What is unique about the application of the process centers around the role of stakeholders—both economic stakeholders, such as customers and suppliers, and those outside the traditional value chain such as communities and the environment. For example, stakeholder discovery means learning to identify stakeholders and the impacts of a company's business on these stakeholders. Impacts might include chemical safety risks, depletion of water resources, noise, and environmental justice for a local community. In many organizations, managers simply may not have considered these issues to be relevant to shareholder value.

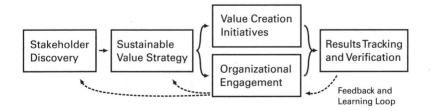

Figure 12-1. The Change Management Process

Phase	Relevant Disciplines	Outcomes
Stakeholder Discovery	*Discipline 1: Understand current value position* *Discipline 2: Anticipate future expectations* Discipline 3: Set sustainable value goals	Managers are able to see the larger system in which the company or unit operates, including economic, social, and environmental dimensions. They have defined key emerging issues and stakeholder impacts relevant to the business.
Sustainable Value Strategy	Discipline 2: Anticipate future expectations *Discipline 3: Set sustainable value goals* Discipline 4: Design value-creation initiatives Discipline 5: Develop the business case	The leadership has a shared vision of value creation for shareholders and stakeholders. An agreed-upon roadmap for how to achieve the vision includes a strategic factbase, goals and objectives, prioritized capacity gaps, value creation initiatives, open issues to address, and stakeholder metrics.
Value-Creation Initiatives	*Discipline 4: Design value-creation initiatives* *Discipline 5: Develop the business case* Discipline 6: Capture the value	Projects and activities are undertaken to create measurable shareholder and stakeholder value in line with the strategy. These projects and activities address supply chain, operations, and customer delivery. They involve key management processes such as how investments are approved and how managers are compensated.
Organizational Engagement	Discipline 5: Develop the business case *Discipline 6: Capture the value* *Discipline 7: Validate results and capture learning* Discipline 8: Build sustainable value capacity	The business unit heads and line managers understand and buy in to the strategy and are clear about what they need to do to achieve it. Value-creation initiatives are implemented with cross-functional teams co-led by line management.
Results Tracking and Verification	*Discipline 7: Validate results and capture learning* *Discipline 8: Build sustainable value capacity (a metadiscipline for all the phases)*	Quantified financial, social, and environmental benefits are tracked with internal and external verification. Benchmarking is conducted relative to peers and relative to emerging sustainability standards (GRI, OECD Guidelines, etc.). The results are effectively communicated to stakeholders.

Figure 12-2. Key Outcomes by Phase

This chapter describes each of the five phases of sustainable value creation and provides examples, tools, and exercises for the practitioner. Key outcomes by phase are shown in Figure 12-2, together with the relevant disciplines discussed in Chapter 11.

Stakeholder Discovery

The discovery phase reassesses our worldview of stakeholders. It requires managers to identify key stakeholder groups and assess the company's economic, social, and environmental impacts on these groups throughout the value chain, much as classic business strategy requires managers to assess the company's financial impacts on shareholders throughout the value chain. In effect, stakeholder value for business represents the market internalization of a social dimension that was viewed as a market externality until recently.

In this phase, assessing stakeholder value is not just about seeing more but about seeing differently. A view of the world centered on sustainable value creation typically involves four key elements that shape how stakeholders are viewed in the business system:

1. *Broad vision:* Seeing all stakeholders in a global systems context
2. *Foresight:* Sensing emerging issues and tracing potential impacts
3. *Deep understanding:* Listening for real concerns and needs
4. *Integrity of action:* Walking the talk to create value, not transfer it

Stakeholder discovery has an information component: providing executives with better and more up-to-date information about emerging issues, such as climate change and the likely price of CO_2 emissions or the implications of the Alien Torts Act for human rights abuses. It also has an experiential and emotional component that transforms how executives relate to social and environmental responsibility. In his new book, *The Heart of Change*,[2] John Kotter says, "People change what they do less because they are given an *analysis* that shifts their *thinking* than because they are *shown* a truth that influences their *feelings*." This observation applies particularly well to the challenge of stakeholder discovery, because this phase requires a deep shift in how businesspeople relate to the world around them. The analytic case for a fuel-cell car, presented in a written document, pales in comparison with actually getting into a quiet, emissions-free vehicle that offers increased safety, comfort, and personalized design—and then imagining how the world would look if all vehicles were like that.

This phase aligns larger issues of sustainability with business purpose. An example of discovery is deep dialogue with stakeholders such as employees and local communities about the company's impacts. Dow Chemical, for instance, listens to its stakeholders through an independent 12-member corporate environmental advisory council whose purpose is to increase understanding of diverse viewpoints through active stakeholder partnership and dialogue.[3]

Social and environmental impacts require the use of different drivers and measures than those used to quantify the financial impacts of a business in the traditional perspective. Ben Cohen, one of the founders of Ben & Jerry's, said, "In a business, the only way to measure success is to count the money you have at the end of the year. Since that is the only thing that is measured, it is the only aim that the people involved in a business are motivated to achieve." In a world where what gets measured gets managed, stakeholder performance requires its own set of metrics.

For many managers who are assessing the shareholder value of social and environmental projects, economic value added and its four drivers (profitability, capital efficiency, cost of capital, and growth) are the most commonly used measures. However, EVA is insufficient for many projects involving emerging issues and stakeholder impacts because of the uncertainty of future cash-flow impacts. Strategic value assessed through real options is a powerful way to account for the *foresight* of management teams in creating opportunities and managing risks from emerging issues that might threaten shareholder value. Market confidence is an intangible influence that can have a large and immediate impact on share price. As noted previously, some portion of market confidence is driven by the overall state of the market and the industry and is not under direct control of management. But to a significant degree, this factor is a reflection of management *integrity*. One of the best measures of a company's management integrity is its track record in stakeholder impacts.

What does the organization look like at the end of the stakeholder discovery phase? If it has done an effective job of assessing current and future stakeholder impacts and value, it knows that it needs to shift strategically, but it doesn't necessarily know what this strategy will look like. The phase of strategy development addresses this next set of objectives.

Strategy Development

The next step is the creation of the sustainable value intent. The competencies and tools needed to create the intent are primarily those of Discipline 3. Once the intent is established, the company needs to develop a strategy to move the business to the win-win quadrant, where value is created for both shareholders and stakeholders. This strategy includes an agreed-upon roadmap for how to achieve the intent. It includes a strategic fact base, goals and objectives, a prioritized set of capacity gaps, a prioritized set of value creation initiatives, open issues to address, and metrics.

Workshops with key managers are supplemented by fact-finding and analysis to identify and assess specific initiatives, identify capability gaps to be filled, and develop an action plan and implementation process.

In strategy development, the key step is to give flesh and bones to the sustainable value vision. Where will business value come from? What

---

SUSTAINABLE VALUE STRATEGY

- What is our sustainable value vision?
- How can we address social impacts, challenges, and future expectations while building business value?
- How should we identify and manage emerging issues?
- How should we measure success?
- What initiatives should we pursue?
- What capabilities do we need?
- How should we proceed?

---

are new sources of sustainable value (that is, where is shareholder value *not* created at the expense of stakeholder value)? Disciplines 3 and 4 are critical to answering these questions.

Value Creation Initiatives

Value creation initiatives convert the vision, plans, and values of a company into tangible results. It is useful to frame the initiatives in terms of levels of strategic focus and financial value drivers that capture the full range of opportunities. The role of strategic value and real options is often overlooked by sustainability champions yet is of heightened interest given the uncertainties of such sustainability-related events as the rise of CO_2 emission permit trading in the future. When Shell invests in solar energy, it is in effect creating a real option for itself in case future markets conditions mandate a rapid move into non-fossil-fuel markets. Disciplines 4 and 5 are the essential competencies here.

Organizational Engagement

Organizational engagement allows key managers to understand and align with the sustainable value creation vision of the senior leadership. Engaging line management is critical to moving the business case from an analytic exercise to specific plans and actions in the business units.

The business world abounds with examples of organizations in which vision statements and value charters are issued by senior executives, only to be ignored by the rest of the organization. I remember one particular day in the fall of 1991 when I visited a sales office of Lafarge in Miami, Florida. As I was sitting in the general sales manager's office, the interoffice mail arrived with a bulky package from headquarters. My host smiled across the desk at me and promptly dumped the package unopened into his wastebasket. He said mailings from headquarters were a waste of time. Imagine if that package had contained a newly formulated strategy for the company with direct consequences for how he was to do his job!

More common are vision statements distributed in interoffice memos or framed on office walls for general consumption. Even if employees do read these declarations of intent, the words have little value beyond the paper they are printed on. For managers to buy into sustainable value creation—particularly managers in business units charged with running the day-to-day operations, who may view anything beyond short-term profit as a distraction from the business of business—they must be given an opportunity to engage in the business logic of stakeholder performance. Organizational alignment is not so much about reinventing the company's strategic intent and developing strategy as it is about grappling with the strategy once senior leadership is aligned.

Shared values reflect the behavioral aspirations of the organization. They are a preferred vehicle for diffusing corporate responsibility throughout the organization. Prescribing behavior or technical compliance to corporate responsibility leads to weak leadership and is often cost-prohibitive. A process to help many employees see the world in a new way enables more profitable integration of corporate responsibility. "What is evoked from within need not be imposed from above." Once employees are aware of and connected to stakeholder concerns, most will naturally try to satisfy them in the conduct of their work—just as when they are aware of customer requirements, they naturally strive to satisfy them.

Shared values relate the whole and the parts—how people, teams, and business units intend to conduct themselves—in pursuit of the company's strategy. They are critical to aligning the business unit managers with the overall direction of the company. At Patagonia, the self-proclaimed dirtbag, sports-oriented culture that grew out of its mountain climbing equipment business in the 1950s helps to focus everyone on the shared environmental and social mission of the company. In other cases, organizational alignment requires a conscious refashioning of focus on a sustainable future—the company's enhanced strategic intent.

By its nature, sustainable value creation requires a cross-functional, cross-border, multilevel engagement of the organization. A guiding coalition composed of senior managers from operations, finance, EH&S,

and one or more sustainability champions is critical to engage the organization in implementing the value creation initiatives. Disciplines 6 and 7 provide the guiding tools to build the organizational engagement needed.

Results Tracking and Verification

If it is true that what gets measured gets managed, then quantifying the benefits of sustainability is one of the essential tasks for EH&S managers and those committed to an integrated bottom line. There are two levels of tracking and verifying results: the project level and the company-wide level. At the project level, benefits are typically cost reductions and materials savings: switching to diesel engines and reducing greenhouse gas emissions while lowering fuel and vehicle maintenance costs, for example, or reengineering a manufacturing process to reduce energy and decrease raw material inputs. At the company-wide level, benefits are more easily related to sustainability brand value, customer mix, and other revenue impacts. The Co-operative Bank (see Chapter 8) provides a good example of a company that has tracked and verified the benefits of ethical, social, and environmental performance at the company-wide level.

In this step, budget priorities that embody the shared values are developed in line with the strategy. The goal is to initiate projects that start delivering value within the fiscal year. Thirty-day, 60-day, and 90-day results are targeted and quantified in financial terms. These are complemented by longer-term projects that enable the firm to advance its financial, environmental, and social performance.

To maximize the benefits of corporate responsibility initiatives, they must be communicated both internally and externally. Companies can develop social responsibility and environmental sustainability reports by using frameworks such as the Global Reporting Initiative, which has been adopted by many leading companies.

CHAPTER THIRTEEN

Surveys of Multinational Companies

S EVERAL SURVEYS have been conducted to find out what companies are doing, or not doing, to create sustainable value. In mid-
2002, the professional services firm PricewaterhouseCoopers (PwC)
canvassed 140 U.S. multinationals for this purpose.[1] The survey results
suggest the surprising extent to which managers are struggling to integrate social and environmental issues into core business practices. Environment, health, and safety managers across a broad range of industries
are not making a credible and compelling business case for sustainability inside their own organizations. This chapter provides further context
for why tool kits are needed, what tools are being asked for, and how
they might be used.

Three-quarters of the PwC survey respondents say they have adopted
some sort of sustainability business practices. The top five practices
cited are pollution prevention (92 percent), environmental management systems (88 percent), employee volunteering (77 percent), community outreach (74 percent), and corporate philanthropy (74 percent).
With the exception of pollution prevention, most of these practices are
not integrated into the value creation process. They represent an end-of-
pipe model of corporate responsibility: environmental or social causes
are addressed after business operations have been fully carried out. This
is obviously true for corporate philanthropy, community outreach, and
employee volunteering, but to some extent it applies also to pollution

prevention (when it is simply a compliance action) and environmental management systems.

A chemical company that produces polymers containing volatile organic compounds can contribute millions of dollars to its favorite charity. In effect, it is transferring value from society to shareholders (by producing products that contribute to harmful ozone formation), and then *re*transferring a part of that value from its shareholders back to society in the form of charity. That is not sustainable value creation.

The British mining company Rio Tinto plc has a long history of extracting value (literally!) at a huge cost to society in such places as Indonesia and Papua New Guinea, while giving a portion of this value back in the form of funding for foundations, scholarships, and corporate philanthropy initiatives aimed at sustainable development. Despite its charities and foundations, Ford Motor Company is leading the marketing charge on extralarge SUVs and lags behind competitors in developing technological alternatives to the combustion engine. To the extent that corporate responsibility is parallel to unsustainable business practices, these cases are not examples of sustainable value creation.

Companies know where to place philanthropy in the scheme of things—it is a transfer of value from shareholders to stakeholders. Philanthropy has a long tradition in the corporate world: U.S. companies gave over $9 billion to nonprofits in 2001. Motives range from intrinsic ("it's the right thing to do") to instrumental ("it enhances the company's reputation"). But corporate giving says nothing about what the company produces, how it produces it, or what its impacts are on its stakeholders. Enron lavished almost $1.5 million on environmental groups that support international energy controls to reduce global warming. From 1994 to 1996, the Enron Foundation contributed large sums to this and other causes.

By contrast, sustainable value is created when a company delivers value to shareholders and stakeholders together in an integrated approach to corporate responsibility. This is what lies at the heart of the business case for ethical, social, and environmental performance. It requires tools and frameworks that allow business managers to identify emerging stakeholder issues, assess the impact of the company's activities on all its stakeholders, measure the business value of relevant corporate responsibility initiatives, and capture that value.

In the PwC survey, 25 percent of respondents said they have not adopted sustainability business practices. Of these, the vast majority (82 percent) cited "no clear business case" as the primary reason. Of all respondents, 72 percent do not incorporate the opportunities or risks associated with sustainability into their business strategies or project, investment, and transaction evaluation processes.

The Belief Gap

In a 2002 survey[2] of 20 companies seen as corporate responsibility leaders (such as Dow Chemical, Dupont, and Hewlett-Packard), the question was asked, "Who inside the company believes in the business value of corporate responsibility?" The managers answering the question were EH&S professionals in the company. Over 80 percent said that they believed in the business value but that less than 40 percent of the financial managers in their companies did. This belief gap between EH&S professionals and finance managers further highlights today's lack of strategic and financial justification for corporate responsibility.

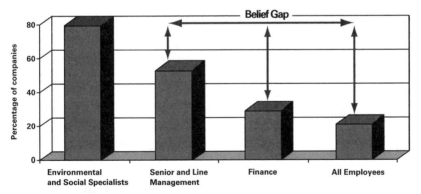

Source: Corporate Responsibility Survey of 20 multinational corporations conducted by Sustainable Value Partners, Inc., in 2002.

Figure 13-1. Survey results show large differences in belief in the business value of beyond-compliance actions. Who inside the company believes in the business value of beyond-compliance environmental and social activities?

When asked, "How do you see corporate responsibility changing in the future in your company?" these same EH&S managers said they see shifting the focus from risk reduction toward creating new business opportunities. They are able to identify the need for more integration of sustainability initiatives into the business units, more accountability and metrics for sustainability performance, and deeper involvement with supply chain issues.

The good news is that EH&S managers now know that the lack of a compelling business case is the primary obstacle to sustainability in their organizations. The previous chapters in Part III are designed to help them begin to make and implement this business case effectively. They offer a follow-through for readers of the book's two earlier parts who might otherwise feel frustrated at the lack of "how-to" in pursuit of tangible results. In this way, Part III responds to the stated concern of readers of recent sustainability books[3] that the helicopter view of new earth-friendly design principles doesn't help their organizations move forward. There is a legitimate concern that high-level sustainability views without guidelines for implementation lead to raised expectations that remain unfulfilled.

Leadership Skills
and the Sustainable Firm

T HERE ARE several things I like about this book, and the most important is that it is bold, a shaper of things to come. Intellectual history suggests that books help a professional's reputation become carved in stone. This is Chris Laszlo's third book of consequence, following his most recent work about changing large, complex organizations.

So what have you learned by reading this complex and honest text about the near future, and how might it influence your next set of decisions? I think you may have learned three things:

1. Some firms are positioned for growth and momentum bets, and a few special firms seem positioned for sustainable growth.

This book is about estimating the value of the difference. Firms such as INNOVEST assert, with good research to back their claim, that key management intangibles are now significant differentiating variables for investment attention and financial reward. INNOVEST further claims that these intangibles consistently differentiate some firms more than 100 basis points above the stock value of their industry-wide competitors, year after year. What Chris Laszlo adds is business savvy, analytic rigor, and organizational common sense about why this is happening and why it is a likely to be a dominant trend for the next decade —not just in Europe and Asia but across the realm of all multinationals, from cement makers to those who sell cosmetics.

From 1995 to 2000, the overall economy grew nearly 7 percent annually, while Enron appeared to grow roughly 32 percent in that same time frame. ("At that rate Enron would have owned the world economy in about 30 years," explains Robert F. Bruner, distinguished professor of business administration at the University of Virginia's Darden Graduate School of Business). Clearly, firms designed for sustainable growth are narrowing their risks and making choices that avoid dangerous results. Risk-taking based on balanced bets is good business, but being at the extreme of a dangerous trend—as the dot-coms, Enron, and WorldCom demonstrate—is not worth the temporary thrill. That's the first key lesson of Chris Laszlo's book and practice, and it's why many people pay attention to the underlying financial approach used in the sustainable value tool kit.

2. Agents of corporate culture change, such as Laszlo, must be bold.

Poison arrow frogs, of infamous use by tribal warriors, make no attempt to blend into the rain forest. They seek open spaces, croak vigorously and constantly, and are not afraid of aggressive arguments in their dense realm of moist green. The same is true of the best book writers on business. They are bold, no matter how gentle their persuasiveness appears at first. Take it from someone, like myself, with five books published since Love Canal.

Chris Laszlo's message about how to align guiding coalitions and how to create a best-options sense of urgency in corporate agendas echoes the lessons on leadership found in the works of many writers, especially John Kotter's 1996 book, *Leading Change.* In addition, this new book advances those classic business arguments with a keen awareness of mounting external threats to future business growth, such as the challenges of climate change; carbon taxes; and the antiglobalization movement that questions, with increasing force, the basic rights of many extractive industries to keep their licenses to operate without significant change. Herman Melville said the seas were his Harvard and Yale; Laszlo and the business book writers that matter seem to give us glimpses into the turbulent seas of corporate change and then provide a steadying effect on the actual decision makers.

3. Competition abounds, even after the demise of the big momentum bets such as Enron. What's left are the sustainable value managers—BP, Lafarge, Anheuser-Busch, Celanese, and Intel—and some of the other market leaders in emerging markets, such as Hewlett-Packard after its tough-love merger with Compaq.

This means that to survive and differentiate themselves, firms must aggressively stand out. Any display of bright color helps the poison arrow frog avoid predator monkeys or birds in its realm. It is the same with firms differentiating through sustainable growth. They plan to thrive, not just survive.

So Why Do We Need Books about Sustainable Firms?

Imagine for 10 minutes what it feels like to run a major multinational like Lafarge, the world's largest cement manufacturing operation, or BP, the petroleum global nexus. To run these fantastically complex intercontinental enterprises requires local smarts and competitive drive, especially during a period of stock performance decline. In such a culture, we need business books that give us hope for a more enduring future. We need these books to avoid future Enrons and to envision a time when we manage our natural resources with intelligence and force.

Decimated by the day-to-day, harassed by audits and congressional investigations, depressed by an erosion of confidence in corporate governance, today's average business leaders might do well to take a vacation with this short, smart book. It will help them prepare better options and next steps.

The Drama and Business Value of Corporate Benchmarking

Benchmarking compares one firm's set of systems to another firm's parallel set of systems. It is an approach to learning for management at a time when learning is critical. *The Sustainable Company* leaps past the many books on sustainable development that are based on concepts alone. I do not need to name them; they are common since the new awareness of environmental and corporate abuse brought on by Love Canal, the *Exxon Valdez,* and Bhopal. What enables this agile step up is Laszlo's corporate experience in benchmarking competitors and his innovative tool kit for the practitioner.

In this book, Laszlo has benchmarked four companies and compared the performance of several hundred. He has helped us notice differences between the sounds, motions, and intentions of some large animals in the marketplace. Why might this prove valuable?

I live in a historic home, built with a stone façade before the American Revolution. In the first 5 years I lived here, I had little time or energy to think about our next set of investments. My family and I felt daily the weight and expense of repairing the past. (I hope most of you can see the parallels for any firm with obligations to remediate historic sites—such obligations may range in the hundreds of millions per year for large petrochemical operations.) But recently, with the weight of those past expenses behind us, I have begun to discern the difference between the sounds a cicada makes in June and the ones a katydid makes in July, the astonishing and resonant nuances that separate the ordinary locust from the refined cricket. You can't see these creatures high in the 200-year-old stand of maple, oak, and black walnut surrounding my house outside of Saratoga, but you can hear them. It is astonishing what one can't hear when pressed by expense, obligation, opportunity, and staffing challenges.

It is the same with corporate benchmarking. At first, you can't see much when you stare into the reflective mirrors of a corporate mansion. The financial statements seem all so self-assured. You ask a tough question, and all you hear is what you heard before. But over time, the sustainable value analyst discerns the short-term winners from those that know how to thrive over time.

The board of directors of a recent multinational client of my firm wanted to be reassured about environmental risks. They wanted to make sure that their environmental management system was second to none, especially when it had to respond urgently and competently to an industrial incident in a densely populated urban area. The challenge was as much about protecting assets and positions as about eliminating the likelihood of misperception by critics or departing investors. So AHC Group members accompanied representatives of that board and their top operations people to five remarkably diverse chemical manufacturers in a six-month period.

To me, what was astonishing is that the client did not operate in the chemical industry. Yet it desired to compare—in a closed, trust-based setting—its risk systems to those deployed by other companies that manage chemical risks. In this benchmarking assignment, our core job was to offer new options for how best to eliminate risk. Chris is drawing on similar assignments. We now call this "real-options analysis and benchmarking."

Chris Laszlo, and his founding partners Dave Sherman and John Whalen, transact this kind of strategic benchmarking in their new AHC Group workshop series called "Near Term Shareholder Value Through Corporate Responsibility," launched in September 2002 with case presentations from leaders at Lafarge, Hewlett-Packard, and the companies joining the World Wildlife Fund in their Climate Savers programs. By mitigating risk and by discerning the value of real improvement options, a refined benchmarking method allows recognition of key field variables. If you read this book with care, you will see a dozen recurrent variables that face and now shape corporate governance.

In sum, a firm needs to learn how to question itself without breaking the bank. Benchmarking for sustainable growth allows that kind of rigorous and rapid learning, with tact at its core. Chris and his team practice what this book preaches.

Bruce Piasecki
President and Founder
American Hazard Control Group

APPENDIX

This appendix provides a reference to a selection of the leading global standards and metrics for social and environmental performance. It contains one global reporting framework (the GRI), three global performance standards (the UN Global Compact, the Sullivan Principles, and the OECD Guidelines), and one socially responsible rating system (INNOVEST). A 2005 ranking of the world's Most Sustainable Companies is provided based on the INNOVEST ratings methodology.

Many other standards and sources of metrics exist, including the Caux Roundtable indicators, SA8000, ISO14000 and ISO14063, AA1000, and new socially responsible investment rating agencies arising in countries around the world.

The Global Reporting Initiative: A Common Framework for Reporting on Economic, Social, and Environmental Performance

The GRI is a long-term, multistakeholder, international institution whose mission is to develop and disseminate globally applicable sustainability reporting guidelines. These guidelines are for voluntary use by organizations to report on the economic, environmental, and social dimensions of their activities, products, and services. The guidelines aim to assist reporting organizations and their stakeholders in articulating and understanding contributions of the reporting organizations to sustainable development. More information about the GRI can be found at http://www.globalreporting.org/GRIGuidelines/index.htm.

The performance indicators used in the GRI framework are grouped into the economic, environmental, and social dimensions and then further structured by category and aspect. For example, biodiversity indicators and transport indicators are listed under environmental reporting aspects. Customer health and safety indicators are listed under product responsibility indicators by social category.

Support is growing for the GRI as a widely accepted disclosure framework for sustainability reporting. It is becoming a concrete expression for social and environmental performance, using both a process and indicators that are moving toward the same standardization that financial accounting acquired in the early decades of the twentieth century.

UN Global Compact: Human Rights, Labor, the Environment

UN Secretary-General Kofi Annan first proposed the Global Compact in an address to the World Economic Forum on January 31, 1999. It became operational in July 2000. The secretary-general challenged business leaders to join an international initiative—the Global Compact—that would bring companies together with UN agencies, labor, and civil society to support nine principles in the areas of human rights, labor, and the environment. These principles can be found by clicking the About GC link at the UN Global Compact home page: http://www.unglobalcompact.org/Portal/.

The Global Sullivan Principles of Social Responsibility

The objectives of the Global Sullivan Principles are to support economic, social and political justice by companies where they do business; to support human rights and to encourage equal opportunity at all levels of employment, including racial and gender diversity on decision making committees and boards; to train and advance disadvantaged workers for technical, supervisory and management opportunities; and to assist with greater tolerance and understanding among peoples; thereby, helping to improve the quality of life for communities, workers and children with dignity and equality.

I urge companies large and small in every part of the world to support and follow the Global Sullivan Principles of Social Responsibility wherever they have operations. (The Reverend Leon H. Sullivan)

As of October 2002, more than 35 leading manufacturing companies, 40 services companies, and 60 professional services firms—as well as numerous business associations and other entities—are signatories to the Global Sullivan Principles. The principles can be found at http:// globalsullivanprinciples.org/principles.htm.

The OECD Guidelines for Multinational Enterprises

These guidelines are nonbinding recommendations to enterprises made by the 37 governments that adhere to them. Their aim is to help multinational enterprises (MNEs) operate in harmony with government policies and with social expectations.

The recommendations provide guidance for appropriate business conduct across the full range of MNE activities. They are supported by implementation procedures in the participating countries, which comprise all 30 OECD member countries and seven nonmember countries (Argentina, Brazil, Chile, Estonia, Israel, Lithuania, and Slovenia). The guidelines can be downloaded in a 55-page document at www.oecd.org/ daf/investment/guidelines/.

INNOVEST: Investment Research in Sustainable Value

INNOVEST is an institutional investment research firm that provides high-quality, comprehensive analysis and best-in-class sector ratings of relative corporate environmental and sustainability performance. INNOVEST differs substantially from the better-known socially responsible investing universe in that it makes no moral judgments, does not manage funds, and does not eliminate or screen major business sectors because of their environmental or social posture. Instead, it examines the effects of industry-wide business drivers of corporate environmental and social policies and specializes in the analysis of how specific companies within these industries are avoiding risks, reducing costs, improving quality, and gaining market share through strategic profit opportunities in the environmental/ sustainability arena.

Led by Jim Martin, former chief investment officer of Teachers Insurance and Annuity Association College Retirement Equities Fund (TIAA-CREF), Hewson Baltzell, a former investment banker, and by founder Dr. Matthew Kiernan, former senior partner of KPMG Peat Marwick, INNOVEST has developed a methodology that rigorously assesses the environmental performance of more than 1,600 global corporations, rates these companies on a scale from AAA to CCC, and then uses this analysis as a proxy for management quality and as a tool to project the stock market returns of these companies. Depending upon the sector, companies with above-average INNOVEST EcoValue'21 ratings have consistently outperformed lower-rated companies by 300 to 1,500 basis points (3 percent to 15 percent) per year. INNOVEST's methodology has been both back-tested and beta tested by Morgan Stanley and PricewaterhouseCoopers. Additionally, a recent quantitative study was done on the INNOVEST research by an independent outside consultant using an APT optimization process, favorably comparing the results of the INNOVEST analysis against the S&P 500 benchmark. Financial clients who use INNOVEST research include T. Rowe Price Associates, Neuberger Berman, Wellington Management, State Street Global Advisors, Lombard Odier, Societe Generale, Rockefeller & Co., and Schroders Investment Management, among others. INNOVEST also does consulting work for the United Nations, U.S. Department of Energy, Environmental Protection Agency, World Bank, National Wildlife Federation, and World Wildlife Fund.

As a result of its research, INNOVEST has been asked to act as subadvisor on portfolios for which the client is interested in professional investment management but also wants the portfolio to reflect environmental and social considerations. INNOVEST acts as subadvisor on $1 billion in investment portfolios whose primary managers include Dreyfus/Mellon Capital, Glenmede Trust Company, Brown Brothers Harriman, and ABN AMRO. Globally, this group of investors includes both institutions and high-net-worth individuals who wish to have their investments not only perform well but also preserve the integrity of the global environment for their children and grandchildren. INNOVEST has found an increasing need for this type of approach with hospitals, religious groups, foundations, and endowments. The INNOVEST research overlay works with any investment style (active, passive, equity, or fixed income), is easy to implement, and requires very little adjustment to the investment approach of investment advisory firms or their portfolio managers.

The Global 100 Most Sustainable Companies Ranked in 2005

The "Global 100 Most Sustainable Corporations in the World" is a projected initiated by Corporate Knights Inc., with INNOVEST Strategic Value Advisors Inc., as the exclusive research analytic data provider. Starting in 2005, the annual "Global 100" will be announced each year at the World Economic Forum in Davos, Switzerland, with the results distributed as a special supplement in the *International Herald Tribune*. The goal of the Global 100 is to encourage and acknowledge those companies willing to pioneer less damaging business methods because if nobody knows which of the players is making progress in this area, it is going to be difficult to maintain the momentum. A company that makes the Global 100 is part of a select group of companies whose sustainability performance falls within the top five percent of their sector, chosen from a universe of 2,000 of the world's largest corporations. Of the 2,000 companies across 53 sectors, the Global 100 are sustainable in the sense that they stand the best chance of being around in 100 years because of their demonstrated performance and strategic ability to manage the triple bottom line (society, environment, and economy).

The Global 100

COMPANY NAME	SECTOR
Alumina Ltd.	Metals and Mining
Dexia	Banks—Europe
RBC Financial Group	Banks—North America
TransAlta Utilities	Electric Utilities—Intl.
Enbridge Inc.	Gas Utilities

COMPANY NAME	SECTOR
Manulife Financial Corp.	Insurance—North America
Sun Life Financial Svcs.	Insurance—North America
Alcan Inc.	Metals and Mining
Vestas Wind Systems A/S	Electrical Equipment
Novo Nordisk A/S	Pharmaceuticals
Nokian Renkaat	Auto Components
Nokia Oyj.	Communications Equipment
Kesko	Food and Drug Retailing
Lafarge SA	Construction Materials
Danone	Food Products
STMicroelectronics	Semiconductor Equipment and Products
Arcelor	Steel
Volkswagen Group	Automobiles
HypoVereinsbank	Banks—Europe
Fresenius Medical Care AG	Health Care Providers and Services
Henkel	Household and Personal Products
Siemens AG	Industrial Conglomerates
Heidelberger Druckmaschinen	Industrial Machinery
SAP AG	Software
Deutsche Telekom	Telecommunications
Adidas Salomon AG	Textiles and Apparel
British Airways Plc.	Airlines
HBOS Plc.	Banks—United Kingdom and Ireland
Diageo	Beverages and Tobacco
SABMiller Plc.	Beverages and Tobacco
Pilkington Plc.	Building Products
Hays Plc.	Commercial Services
DS Smith Plc.	Containers and Packaging
3i Group Plc.	Diversified Financials—United Kingdom
Scottish and Southern Energy Plc.	Electric Utilities—Intl.

COMPANY NAME	SECTOR
Expro International Group	Energy Equipment and Services
J Sainsbury Plc.	Food and Drug Retailing
Cadbury Schweppes Plc.	Food Products
Unilever	Food Products
Centrica Plc.	Gas Utilities
Smith & Nephew	Health Care Equipment and Supplies
Taylor Woodrow Plc.	Homebuilding
Whitbread Plc.	Hotels, Restaurants, and Leisure
AVIVA	Insurance—United Kingdom and Ireland
BP Plc.	Integrated Oil and Gas
GUS Plc.	Multiline Retail
Marks & Spencer Plc.	Multiline Retail
Cairn Energy Plc.	Oil and Gas Exploration and Production
GlaxoSmithKline Plc.	Pharmaceuticals
Severn Trent Plc.	Public Services
Pearson Plc.	Publishing
British Land Company Plc.	Real Estate
Land Securities Plc.	Real Estate
Slough Estates Plc.	Real Estate
Kingfisher Plc.	Specialty Retail
BAA Plc.	Surface Transport
Penninsular and Oriental Steam Navigation Co.	Surface Transport
BT Group Plc.	Telecommunications
DESNO	Auto Components
Toyota Motor Corp.	Automobiles
Kuraray Company, Ltd.	Commodity Chemicals
Ricoh Company, Ltd.	Electronic Equipment and Instruments
NTT DoCoMo Inc.	Telecommunications
ABN AMRO Holding	Banks—Europe

COMPANY NAME	SECTOR
ING Group	Diversified Financials—Europe
Philips Electronics	Household Durables
Royal Dutch Petroleum Co.	Integrated Oil and Gas
Reed Elsevier Plc.	Publishing
TOMRA Systems ASA	Industrial Machinery
Gamesa Corporacion Tecnologica SA	Industrial Machinery
Indra Sistemas	IT Consulting and Services
FoereningsSparbanken AB	Banks—Europe
Ericsson	Communications Equipment
Skanska	Construction and Engineering
Volvo Group	Construction and Farm Machinery
Electrolux AB	Household Durables
Svenska Cellulosa AB	Paper and Forest Products
Hennes & Mauritz	Specialty Retail
ABB AG	Electrical Equipment
Swiss Reinsurance Company	Insurance—Europe
United Technologies Corp.	Aerospace and Defense
United Postal Service	Air Freight and Couriers
Bank of America	Banks—North America
PepsiCo Inc.	Beverages and Tobacco
Pitney Bowes	Commercial Services and Supplies
Hewlett-Packard Company	Computers and Peripherals
FPL Group Inc.	Electric Power Companies—North America
Pinnacle West Capital Corp.	Electric Power Companies—North America
Agilent	Electronic Equipment and Instruments
Xerox Corp.	Electronic Equipment and Instruments
Schlumberger Ltd.	Energy Equipment and Services
Baxter International Inc.	Health Care Equipment and Supplies

COMPANY NAME	SECTOR
Marriott International, Inc. (New)	Hotels, Restaurants, and Leisure
Eastman Kodak Co.	Leisure Equipment and Products
Alcoa Inc.	Metals and Mining
Weyerhaeuser Co.	Paper and Forest Products
Bristol-Myers Squibb Co.	Pharmaceuticals
Intel Corp.	Semiconductor Equipment and Products
Ecolab Inc.	Specialty Chemicals
AT&T Corp.	Telecommunications

List published with permission from Corporate Knights Inc., and INNOVEST Strategic Value Advisors Inc.

NOTES

Chapter 2

1. Ross Gelbspan, *The Heat Is On* (Cambridge, Mass.: Perseus Publishing, 1998), 171.

2. William McDonough and Michael Braungart, *Cradle-to-Cradle: Remaking the Way We Make Things* (New York: North Point Press, 2002).

3. Quoted in Carl Frankel, *In Earth's Company: Business, Environment and the Challenge of Sustainability* (Gabriola Island, B.C., Canada: New Society Publishers, 1998), p. 113.

4. *Ibid.*, 13.

5. *Earth Island Journal* (U.S), Spring 1997; *Ethical Consumer* (UK), February/ March 1997.

6. Laara Lindo and Yasuhiko Kimura, eds., *THINK, The First Principle of Business Ethics: Excerpts from the Legendary IBM Lecture Series by Walter Russell*, with a foreword by Chris Laszlo and a personal introduction by Thomas J. Watson, Sr. (Waynesboro, Va.: The University of Science and Philosophy, 2003).

7. Frankel, 1998.

8. Auden Schendler, "Where's the Green in Green Business?" *Harvard Business Review*, June 2002.

Chapter 3

1. INNOVEST, KLD, and TSI (United States), Core Ratings (France), Avanzi (Italy), Caring Company (Sweden), CentreInfo (Switzerland), FED (Spain), Jantzi (Canada), PIRC (UK), Scoris (Germany), Triodos (Netherlands), and SIRIS (Australia) are just some of the SRI rating agencies using these sustainability benchmarks.

Chapter 4

1. Lawrence Weinbach, Unisys Chairman, quoted in Jeffrey Garten, *The Mind of the CEO* (Cambridge, Mass.: Perseus Publishing, 2002).

2. Cited in James E. Post, et al., *Redefining the Corporation: Stakeholder*

Management and Organizational Wealth (Stanford, Calif.: Stanford University Press, 2002), 27.

3. Dennis Minano, former chief environmental officer at General Motors, as relayed to the author in a personal conversation at the AHC Group meeting in Saratoga Springs, N.Y., in June 2002.

Chapter 5

1. James E. Post et al., *Redefining the Corporation: Stakeholder Management and Organizational Wealth* (Stanford, Calif.: Stanford University Press, 2002).

2. Paul Ray and Sherry Anderson, *The Cultural Creatives: How 50 Million People Are Changing the World* (New York: Harmony Books, 2000).

3. Neva Goodwin, "A Revolution in Values," *Human Environment* 5(2), Spring 1998.

4. Cited in Andrew Hoffman, *Competitive Environmental Strategy* (Washington, D.C.: Island Press, 2000), 86, 87.

Chapter 6

1. The Patagonia story told here is based in part on the author's participation at Michael Crooke's presentation of his company at the Harvard Business School on March 2, 2002. Other sources include the company's own reports, as well as the excellent chapter in Lorinda R. Rowledge, Russell S. Baron, and Kevin S. Brady, *Mapping the Journey: Case Studies in Developing and Implementing Sustainable Development Strategies* (Sheffield, UK: Greenleaf Publishing Ltd., 1999). I would also like to thank John Whalen for first bringing to my attention the transformative experience of the company's San Joaquin Valley tour in 1992.

2. Quoted in *Mapping the Journey.*

Chapter 7

1. The ARCO chapter was cowritten with Kenneth Dickerson, former senior vice president of external affairs at ARCO. As I have drawn on multiple sources of information, any inaccuracies about this case are mine.

2. Forest Reinhardt, *Down to Earth: Applying Business Principles to Environmental Management* (Cambridge, Mass.: Harvard Business Press, 2000), 75.

Chapter 8

1. The Co-operative Bank, *Partnership Report 2001: Our Impact,* 11.

2. FTSE4Good is an enhanced stock market index like the Dow Jones Sustainability Group Index.

3. The Co-operative Bank, 90.

Chapter 10

1. Stakeholder value is measured *relative to absolute standards* and *relative to peers.* By absolute standards, we mean those that meet the (generally scientific) tests for stakeholder well-being or for sustainability as a capacity for continuance. An example given in Chapter 12 distinguishes absolute standards and those relative to an industry average.

2. John Lippert, "Toyota Plans All Gas-Electric Vehicles by 2012," *Bloomberg News,* in *Auto Industry News,* October 25, 2002.

3. See, for example, Lawrence Burns et al., "Vehicle of Change," *Scientific American* 287(4), October 2002.

4. The ROE of the automobile industry in 1998 was 13.4 percent, compared to 17.1 percent for the S&P 500.

5. Roger Schreffler, "Toyota Moving Quickly with Hybrid Technology," AP, August 7, 2001.

6. See, for example, "Fuel-Cell Cars Take to California Roads," *Road & Track*, January 2003.

7. The Prius's tag line is "Prius/genius," showing "not only the intelligence of the new technology but also the creative web-based marketing approach."

8. John Low and Pam Cohen Kalafut, "The Invisible Advantage," *Optimize,* June 2002 (online at http://www.optimizemag.com/issue/008/roi.htm).

9. See the Appellate Court cases of Mississippi farmer Homer McFarling or Saskatchewan farmer Percy Schmeiser.

10.Frankel, 90, 91.

11. Post et al., 17.

Chapter 11

1. Six Sigma is a business process focused on streamlining operations, improving quality, and eliminating mistakes. It has been widely adopted by the Global 1000 companies.

2. Chris Laszlo and Jean-Francois Laugel, *Large Scale Organizational Change: An Executive's Guide* (Woburn, Mass.: Butterworth-Heinemann, 2000).

Chapter 12

1. For a classic work by Peter Drucker that covers many of the change-management processes of Chapter 13, see *Managing for Results: Economic Tasks and Risk-Taking Decisions* (New York: HarperBusiness, 1993, reprint).

2. John Kotter, *The Heart of Change: Real-Life Stories of How People Change Their Organizations* (Cambridge, Mass.: Harvard Business Press, 2002).

3. Presentation by Sam Smolnik, EH&S vice president, Dow Chemical, at the AHC Group in June 2002.

Chapter 13

1. PricewaterhouseCoopers, *2002 Sustainability Survey Report,* August 2002.

2. Sustainable Value Partners private workshop survey, September-October 2002.

3. For example, see Amazon.com reader reviews of McDonough and Braungart.

FURTHER READING

Articles

Austin, Duncan, and Amanda Sauer. 2002. *Changing Oil: Emerging Environmental Risks and Shareholder Value in the Oil and Gas Industry.* Washington, D.C.: World Resources Institute.

Blumberg, J., Å. Korsvold, and G. Blum. 1996. *Environmental Performance and Shareholder Value.* Geneva: World Business Council for Sustainable Development.

Gilding, Paul, Murray Hogarth, and Don Reed. 2002. *Single Bottom Line Sustainability: How a Value Centered Approach to Corporate Sustainability Can Pay Off for Shareholders and Society.* Sydney: Ecos Corporation.

Global Environmental Management Initiative. 1998. *Environment: Value to Business.*

Global Environmental Management Initiative. 2001. *Environment: Value to the Top Line.* Focuses on revenues, market share growth, brand reputation, and share price.

Holliday, Chad, and John Pepper. 2001. "Sustainability Through the Market: Seven Keys to Success." Geneva: World Business Council for Sustainable Development.

Innovest Strategic Value Advisors. 2002. *Value At Risk: Climate Change and the Future of Governance.* Boston: Coalition for Environmentally Responsible Economies. One of the best reports on the direct links among climate change, fiduciary responsibility, and shareholder value.

Laszlo, Chris. 2002. "Measuring and Managing Corporate Responsibility." *Ethical Corporation Magazine* (April-May). A view from the capital markets.

Laszlo, Chris, David Sherman, and John Whalen. 2002. "Shareholder Value and Corporate Responsibility." *Ethical Corporation Magazine* (December).

Manley, Mark. 2002. "Risking Shareholder Value? Exxon Mobil and Climate Change." 2002. Claros Discussion Paper.

Prahalad, C. K., and Stuart L. Hart. 2001. "The Fortune at the Bottom of the Pyramid." *Strategy+Business* (no. 26).

Reed, Donald J. 2001. *Stalking the Elusive Business Case for Corporate Sustainability.* Washington, D.C.: World Resources Institute.

"Survey: The Global Environment." *The Economist,* July 6, 2002. This article provides an excellent introduction to sustainable development.

Books

Daily, Gretchen C. 2002. *The New Economy of Nature.* Washington, D.C.: Island Press.

Hoffman, Andrew J. 2000. *Competitive Environmental Strategy: A Guide to the Changing Business Landscape.* Washington, D.C.: Island Press.

Holliday, Chad, Stephan Schmidheiny, and Philip Watts. 2002. *Walking the Talk: The Business Case for Sustainable Development.* Sheffield, UK: Greenleaf Publishers.

Kemp, Vicky. 2001. *To Whose Profit? Building a Business Case for Sustainability.* Surrey, UK: World Wildlife Fund–UK.

McDonough, William, and Michael Braungart. 2002. *Cradle-to-Cradle: Remaking the Way We Make Things.* New York: North Point Press.

Nattrass, Brian, and Mary Altomare. 1999. *The Natural Step for Business: Wealth, Ecology and the Evolutionary Corporation.* Gabriola Island, B.C., Canada: New Society Publishers.

Piasecki, Bruce, et al. 1999. *Environmental Management and Business Strategy: Leadership Skills for the 21st Century.* John Wiley.

Post, James, Lee Preston, and Sybille Sachs. 2002. *Redefining the Corporation: Stakeholder Management and Organizational Wealth.* Stanford, Calif.: Stanford University Press.

Reinhardt, Forest. 1999. *Down to Earth: Applying Business Principles to Environmental Management.* Cambridge, Mass.: Harvard Business Press.

Repetto, Robert, and Duncan Austin. 2000. *Pure Profit: The Financial Implications of Environmental Performance.* Washington, D.C.: World Resources Institute.

Rowledge, Lorinda R., Russell S. Barton, and Kevin S. Brady. 1999. *Mapping the Journey: Case Studies in Strategy and Action Toward Sustainable Development.* Sheffield, UK: Greenleaf Publishing.

Svendsen, Ann. 1998. *The Stakeholder Strategy: Profiting from Collaborative Business Relationships.* San Francisco: Berrett-Koehler.

Willard, Bob. 2002. *The Sustainability Advantage.* Gabriola Island, B.C., Canada: New Society Publishers.

ABOUT THE AUTHOR

Chris Laszlo is partner and cofounder of Sustainable Value Partners, Inc., a firm that specializes in creating shareholder value through corporate responsibility. For nearly 10 years, Chris was an executive of Lafarge S.A., a world leader in building materials, where he held positions as head of strategy, general manager of a manufacturing subsidiary, and vice president of business development. Before that, he spent 5 years with Deloitte & Touche, where he provided strategy consulting services to such global industry leaders as Dupont, Toshiba, Avon Products, and Renault.

He received his Ph.D. in economics and management science from the University of Paris, a Master's in economics from Columbia University, and a B.A. from Swarthmore College. He has authored management books including *Large Scale Organizational Change: An Executive's Guide* (with Jean-Francois Laugel, Butterworth-Heinemann, 2000) and *The Insight Edge: An Introduction to the Theory and Practice of Evolutionary Management* (with Ervin Laszlo, Quorum Books, 1997).

INDEX